For my fabulous family and friends, who inspire me, love me and support me every day. THANK YOU X

the VINTAGE TEA PARTY book

ANGEL STRAWBRIDGE

MITCHELL BEAZLEY

For Arthur and Dorothy. You melt my heart and make
me laugh every day. You are my world.

For my best friend Dick. Thank you for being the most
incredible husband and daddy. I love our lives - even
our arguments!

For my mum and dad, family and friends who inspire
and support me every day. Thank you.

The Vintage Tea Party Book by Angel Adoree
First published in Great Britain in 2011 by Mitchell Beazley,
an imprint of Octopus Publishing Group Limited,
Carmelite House, 50 Victoria Embankment, London, EC4Y 0DZ
www.octopusbooks.co.uk

This edition published in 2018

An Hachette UK Company | www.hachette.co.uk
Copyright © Octopus Publishing Group Limited 2011, 2018 | Text copyright © Angel Adoree 2011, 2018

Note: This book contains some dishes made with raw or lightly cooked eggs. It is prudent for more vulnerable people such as pregnant and nursing mothers, invalids, the elderly, babies and young children to avoid dishes made with uncooked or lightly cooked eggs.

Photographers Yuki Sugiura (food & drink); David Edwards (projects & locations) | Illustrator Adele Mildred | Back Cover Illustrator Michael Petherick | Stylist Angel Adoree | Food Stylist Sue Henderson | Ass. Food Stylist Jon Stewart | Copy-editor Alison Copland | Proofreader Salima Hirani | Indexer Helen Snaith | Senior Production Controller Caroline Alberti | Senior Editor Leanne Bryan | Editorial Director Eleanor Maxfield | Art Director & Designer Yasia Williams-Leedham

ISBN: 978 1 78472 567 9
A CIP catalogue record for this book is available from the British Library.
Set in Reminga, Gorey, Justlefthand and Lady Rene.
Printed and bound in China.

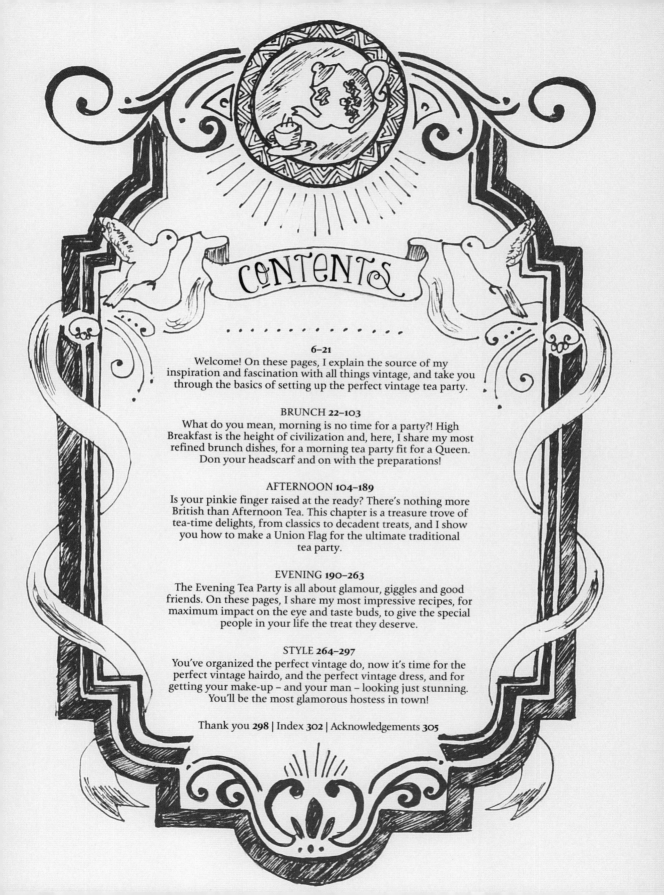

CONTENTS

PAST, PRESENT & FUTURE

Welcome to *The Vintage Tea Party Book*. You are about to embark on an imaginative journey to create your perfect tea party. The pages ahead of you capture my passion and fantasy for all things vintage and I feel incredibly blessed that I've been given the opportunity to share this with you.

This book is divided into five chapters: this introduction, Brunch, Afternoon, Evening and Style. To use the book:

1 Decide when your tea party will be held and select your favourite recipes and features from the main chapters to incorporate.

2 Use the introduction and Style chapters to elevate your party into the full vintage experience.

3 Eat, drink, love, laugh and keep the memory for ever.

Above: My dad (centre) playing the Mad Hatter in his school play, 1959.

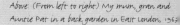

Above: (From left to right) My mum, gran and Auntie Pat in a back garden in East London, 1967.

Right: Nan caught having a sneaky cigarette in an East London alley, 1951.

My Journey

I like old things. Unique one-off items with character and charm. Old-fashioned rituals, manners and ways of life define me. I live and breathe a past time when life was simpler, yet steeped in style and elegance.

I discovered my passion for all things vintage when I was just a few years old. My family is from the East End of London and I was brought up by ladies whom I considered to be the most beautiful and elegant in all the land! My family is very open-hearted and were always throwing soirées when I was younger.

We have always worked hard as a family, but we know the importance of family time and this always revolves around food! My early experiences, shared with them around the dining table, at the kitchen counter and on many a picnic blanket, are the source of my passion for entertaining.

During my teens, I started thrifting at a local car boot sale and became addicted to hunting down glamorous old items. I would buy clothes that did not fit, tea sets I would not use and a variety of other items that cluttered up my room and sent my parents into a spin! In my early twenties, I transformed my addiction into my first business, called the Angel-A Vintage Experience. I would sell my finds while spoiling my guests with wonderful food and drink. As I mentioned, hosting is part of my being and, in 2007, my humble beginnings in vintage hospitality took the natural progression into a fully-fledged vintage hospitality business. The Vintage Patisserie was born, offering bespoke vintage parties. I had to pinch myself every day at the fact that I was making people happy by indulging in my passion!

Right: Designer Erdem and the Vintage Patisserie team at the Cutler and Gross Vintage store, 2009.

In 2010, my love of business and vintage also led me to apply for 'Dragons' Den'. The Dragons were very nice and apparently the TV liked me! I was signed by an agent who happened to be the agent of Dick Strawbridge... The rest, as they say, is history.

In 2013, Dick And I were blessed with Arthur Donald Strawbridge and in 2014, Dorothy Francis Strawbridge! Life changed and Dick and I wanted to give our children the world. The search for a different life got serious.

The Present

Dick and I talked long and hard about work–life balance and finally made the decision to buy a little chateau in France to concentrate on hosting fabulous vintage events, something that is very close to both our hearts. We captured our journey on Channel 4's 'Escape to the Chateau'. It's been an incredible experience and we look forward to watching it with the children in years to come!

Clockwise from below: Family Strawbridge on our wedding day at Chateau de la Motte Husson, 2016.

Thank you for choosing to come on this journey with me – I'd like to raise
a glass to you.

'To your perfect tea party. May it bring health, happiness, love and lots of laughter.'

Love Angel ♡

LOCATION

Whether it's tea for two or two hundred, finding the right location is essential for creating your perfect tea party. As a host and events organizer, I always start by asking myself the following questions:

Who am I hosting? ❧ How many am I hosting? ❧ What first impression am I trying to create? ❧ Do I want to hold the party in a themed building?

Home

Never rule out the most obvious solution. We all know that the most memorable parties are in our friends' homes. This is partly because the host is comfortable and relaxed, which creates that personal magic. There are no worries about closing times or logistics, and it's your home! No other place will emulate that intimacy and openness. If you want the personal touch but you have concerns about space, fear not. Think about utilizing outdoor space. Most parties, even tea parties, are not seated. There is a wealth of specialist companies on your doorstep that can help with furniture, marquees, outdoor lighting and heating – most are local businesses with the personal touch and they will work within your budget.

That spare room on top of that great pub that no one knows about

If your home is not the answer, then go exploring. At times like this, I look for a location first: somewhere accessible for everyone is a good starting point. Then, equipped with my favoured lipstick and smile, I go hunting. Bars, restaurants, clubs, pubs, churches, town halls... any venue with character gets a visit. Asking is the key. You'll be surprised at how many places have an upstairs room or a secret back room that is not often used. Try looking around your nearest financial district – areas like these are heaving in the week, but at the weekend are like ghost towns, which is perfect for striking a good deal.

The great outdoors

If the great outdoors is more your cup of tea, then try your local park, the gardens of an exquisite stately home or your local riverside. If you like the idea of hosting a party in the park, there may be some rules and regulations that you will have to follow before you start handing out the cakes, so get in contact with your local authority in advance to ask permission and to see if there are any fees for holding a party there. They may even tell you of some places you don't know about.

On the go

How about having a party on the go? Hire a vintage bus, an old-fashioned double decker, or even a taxi (yes, I have hosted a tea party in a black cab). The only things you'll have to worry about are the food, drink and china, and having a good time. There are many original buses still around that aren't being used. If you're feeling really adventurous, try hosting on a boat or even in an original World War II aircraft. This could be a bit tricky for space, but your party will be talked about for ages!

THE INVITATION

I have 2,500 friends, according to a social-networking website I frequent.

I've often wondered, if I were to invite them all over to my house for dinner, how many would come. Would I send a group email or create an event online and invite them through that? Of the people that came, how many would be my friends? Some people might come just to taste my delights and have a peek at my fabulous shoe collection!

My guess is that the party would be full of people I know by face but not by name. Although that could be the start of a rather interesting evening, it's the opposite of what makes my gatherings memorable.

I love a bit of social networking as much as the next vintage-clad lass, and I enjoy getting a reminder when its someone's birthday and finding out what people ate for dinner or if they have had a smelly person sitting next to them on public transport, but it will never be a substitute for the connection that you have when you are laughing and sharing with someone, and being together.

Call me old-fashioned, but I like to clutch on to bits of the past that I think are rather charming. I talk to my family and friends on the phone, and sometimes see them face to face. This direct contact will always be more precious than any website.

In an age when we seemingly have far less physical connection than in times past, I like to make every gathering as special as I possibly can – not just in the moment, but also in the lead-up, the preparation, the connection, the ending and the thank yous.

I start every occasion with an invitation for the selected one to join my journey. An invitation is not just for communicating the facts of where and when (although it's very important to include these). It also sets the tone for the entire party.

I'll never tire of receiving a handwritten invitation. I get a little kick of adrenaline as I open the envelope, not knowing what's to come. I can usually tell, though, from how the piece of paper is inscribed, what is expected of me, and I'm always thrilled to be taking part in the sender's journey.

It makes me smile to know that someone has taken the time to handwrite something and include me. That personal touch should be the start of your journey too.

Yes, I'm defiantly old-fashioned for all the right reasons.

On the pages that follow are some ready-made invitations. Feel free to photocopy them to use as your own, or download them from www.vintagepatisserie.co.uk.

YOU HAVE BEEN INVITED

BY

YOU HAVE BEEN
BY INVITED

You Have Been Invited

By ....

SOURCING
PROPS

1 A cast-metal, tole and
polychrome-painted birdcage,
ith scroll-turned cresting over
domed body, set with fruiting
ne leaves and stylized leaf-
ailed borders, 1920s.

2 A black-glazed and parcel-
gilt teapot and cover, with
boldly striped globular body and
ylized leaf-trailed borders, 1920s.

3 A lustre china teacup
and saucer, the trumpet-
aped cup with a broad gilt rim,
ainted with roses inside, with
bed saucer, 1970s.

4 A small Charlie Chaplin
figurine raised on a
aluster-turned stem set within a
ass-domed cloche, 1930s.

5 Two vintage leather
suitcases, inscribed with
he owner's initials (V.C.P.) circa
940s/50s.

6 A black-and-white silk
evening dress, with broad-cut
ecolletage inset with sequins, 1930s.

7 A vintage Union Jack
flag, 1940s.

8 A taxidermy owl in a
lacquered wood and bevelled
ass showcase, circa late 19th/early
oth century.

The first time I bought a tea set, from a local boot fair, I was just 12 years old. I had no use for it, but it was very cheap and rather fabulous. Even at that age I remember thinking 'I can sell it at a later date'. And I did, ten years later! Summer 1990 was the start of my career and I never knew it. 'Thrifting' is still my favourite pastime, so here are a few tips on sourcing the goods to ensure you get the right bits at the right price. Remember: if you like it, get it. You may never come across another one.

Vintage is not a new concept
Throughout the 20th century, many fashion designers took their inspiration from the past. In the 1920s, Jeanne Lanvin created ultra-feminine dresses inspired by the French Second Empire (19th century), which were already then referred to as 'vintage'. In the 1960s and 1970s, Barbara Hulanicki created romantic garments for women, in contrast to the futuristic styles and brightness of the contemporary clothing. Her designs were also described as 'vintage', finding their inspiration in past times.

Be innovative; buy 'against the grain'
If you want to make good investments, or find bargains, follow your own creative taste and buy what others don't buy. As long as the quality and decoration are fine, your choice should be quite safe. Even though vintage items are extremely popular at the moment, there are still a great many treasures unfound and untouched. Be adventurous in your choice.

Where to buy
There are plenty of places where you can find vintage items. Antique shops, auction houses (especially generalist uncatalogued sales), car-boot/garage sales, charity shops and internet selling platforms are all good places for buying vintage. The best bargains can be obtained when vintage items are offered outside a 'vintage' context, and thus get a bit lost among other items. Therefore don't necessarily look for vintage sales, but expand your search and try to spot that special item within a wider remit; as probably no one else will have noticed it.

Condition
Of paramount importance when buying vintage is the condition of the piece. There's no point buying vintage porcelain or glass if you have to spend twice the purchase price to have it restored. Besides, there are very few good restorers and they are often very busy. Watch out for cracks and previous repairs. If you discover the item has been previously damaged, just don't buy it. As vintage items are not that old compared to other antiques, vintage collectors are (more than in any other collecting field) very particular and want the items to be in overall good condition commensurate with their age.

Furniture

Do you fancy late 1940s American furniture? Do you like 20th-century design, or even pre-war chairs? Designer furniture from the previous century, such as Charles and Ray Eames chairs, have often been 'edited' throughout recent decades. Therefore, where original furniture from the 1930s, 1940s and 1950s might be very expensive to purchase, do consider buying later editions, as these can prove to be far less expensive; when they have acquired a bit of wear and tear, they can have as much impact as the originals.

Vintage clothes

There many places where you can buy vintage clothes. Bear in mind that an increasing number of auction houses now have a department dedicated to fashion, where you will find not only highly wearable evening dresses, but also a lot of designer clothes at attractive prices. You can mix and match some of these vintage clothes to enhance the stylish effect and create your unique look. If you buy well-known vintage fashion labels, the value should also remain or even go up after a few years, further proving it might be a worthwhile investment.

Porcelain

During the 19th and 20th centuries, porcelain tea services were frequently given to young couples as wedding presents. These were kept at the time in dedicated display cabinets and only used on special occasions. They have therefore survived in huge quantities and are often in very good condition. The market is currently flooded with large sets of tea services dating back to the late 19th and early 20th centuries. Because these porcelain tea services are not very fashionable in the current market, it is definitely the right time to buy and enjoy them.

Silver cutlery

Both solid silver and electroplate cutlery have marks, which can often be misleading. On British electroplated silver, you will find the marks EP, EPNS or EPBM. You can also identify electroplated silver if the base metal is showing through. Electroplated silver is very expensive when bought new, but in a secondary market it can be very good value and is extremely decorative when in good condition. Silver usually bears four or five marks: maker's mark, lion passant, town mark, date letter and, sometimes, a duty mark. Again it is a good time to buy silver – not many young people tend to purchase it, as it can be seen as old-fashioned and needs cleaning.

Tea party checklist

Essentials: Teapots, teacups and saucers, dessert plates, cake plates, cakestands, milk jugs, sugar bowls, glassware and jugs, dessert forks, knives, teaspoons, serving spoons.

Non-essentials: Vintage card games, dominos, draughts (boards and pieces), taxidermy, Union Jack, World War II memorabilia – especially flags, tins, candleholders, gramophones, cameras and anything weird and wonderful that catches your eye!

9 An octagonal lacquered tole box, with ivory ground reserves decorated with Egyptian-inspired scenes and the cover with lotus-blossom motifs, circa 1920–40.

10 A parcel-gilt 'pink' sadler teapot, with stylized sinuous line motifs on a coral ground, 1970s.

11 A miniature Charlie Chaplin memorabilia doll, featuring Charlie in traditional costume holding an umbrella, 1930s.

12 An Indian metal moulded three-tier travel tazza set, featuring three circular dishes emanating from a hoop, raised on a bell-shaped base, early 20th century.

13 A Victorian electroplate James Deakin egg coddler, of ovoid shape, with chicken cast finial and a triform openwork stand, 1871.

14 A stoneware jelly and potted-meat mould, with a brown-glazed exterior of oval lobed shape raised on a flaring base, 1860s.

Jelly and
Potted
Meat
Mould

kitchen ATMOSPHERE

No one can deny that a cake baked with love tastes better than a cake baked under pressure. Here are my tips for ensuring your party goes to plan and that you enjoy the entire process.

1 On the day of your gathering, make sure you are organized and that you know what your cooking timeline is. Always give yourself 25 per cent extra time.

2 If you are catering for the masses, ask your friends for help. It will be fun and the perfect chance to catch up on the latest goings-on.

3 Make sure you are prepped (*see* Style, pages 264–297). All vintage hairstyles start with some sort of curl, and leaving it for the day gives it the best chance to set.

4 Wear a headscarf for style (and hygiene purposes) and put your best cooking music on to feed the soul. You should now be ready!

Tying the Perfect Headscarf

To get a quick and easy 1940s daytime look, here is a step-by-step example for you lovely ladies. You can wear it just to keep your hair up or to keep your curlers in. It will make you look every inch the 1940s land girl.

1 Firstly, clip up the back of your hair with hair grips. Try to get it as flat as you can so that it doesn't create a bump when you put your headscarf on. You can leave your fringe out if you want to curl it after you've secured your scarf.

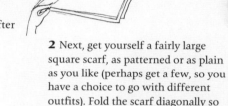

2 Next, get yourself a fairly large square scarf, as patterned or as plain as you like (perhaps get a few, so you have a choice to go with different outfits). Fold the scarf diagonally so you have a triangle.

3 With the middle point of the triangle facing towards the front of your head, place the folded scarf on your hair, holding the other two points of the scarf in either hand.

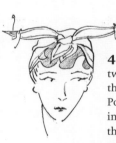

4 Now tie a knot with the two points of the scarf that you are holding. Position the knot in the middle of the scarf, so it sits neatly on top of the middle point.

5 The middle point can be rolled in with the knot so it is unnoticeable. Ladies like variation so, depending on how big your scarf is, you can tie the knot as small or as big as you like.

6 Once it's knotted, secure it with as many hair grips as you find necessary – usually three or four will hold it perfectly in place. Any hanging bits of scarf can also be hidden away with grips or slipped under the scarf.

BRUNCH

BRUNCH CONTENTS

There is something about a breakfast tea party that cannot be captured at any other time of the day.

Our body clocks are not programmed to be having a fabulous time so early, fresh-faced and hungry, and this always leaves me feeling a little naughty and rather indulgent. I'm a fan of the unexpected, and High Breakfast is my secret weapon for wooing my loved ones.

I always nod at tradition, including oats, fruit, eggs, meat, fish, bread and spreads and of course a quick headscarf. And my morning cooking recipes are quick, easy and delicious to ensure I get as much beauty sleep as possible beforehand.

IMPORTANT WARNING: Be careful when making this recipe as you will discover that no shop-bought granola will ever satisfy you or your pocket again. Once you have tried my Chocolate Coconut Granola, you will see how simple it is to make and thereafter you will only be limited by your imagination.

CHOCOLATE COCONUT GRANOLA

PREP
10 minutes

COOKING
1¼ hours

SERVES 8

240g (8½oz) rolled oats
175g (6oz) flaked almonds
70g (2½oz) shredded unsweetened coconut
70g (2½oz) dark brown sugar
40g (1½oz) unsweetened cocoa powder
90ml (3fl oz) honey
50ml (2fl oz) vegetable oil
1 tsp ground cinnamon
¾ tsp salt

1 Preheat the oven to 120°C/fan 100°C/gas mark ½.

2 In a large bowl, mix the oats, almonds, coconut and brown sugar. In a separate bowl, mix the cocoa powder, honey, oil, cinnamon and salt.

3 Combine the 2 mixtures and pour on to 2 baking sheets. Bake the granola for 1¼ hours, stirring every 15 minutes to achieve an even colour.

4 Transfer to a large bowl to serve.

Vintage glassware is incredibly easy to pick up if you are not looking for an entire set. I fall in love every time I get myself a new gold-edged glass, and what better way to make use of your new purchases and delight your friends than this ridiculously simple-to-make take on an ice-cream sundae? The flavours are fresh and creamy and make every mouthful a pleasure. Greek yogurt and honey are a must, but you can be as experimental as you like with the rest of the ingredients. Why not add some of my Orange and Lemon Curd (*see* page 84)? And for the crunch (which is a must for texture) add Chocolate Coconut Granola (*see* page 26) or nuts.

FRUIT SUNDAE

PREP
5 minutes

MAKES
8 small vintage glasses

150g (5½oz) raspberries

150g (5½oz) blueberries

150g (5½oz) blackberries

500g (1lb 2oz) Greek yogurt

90ml (3fl oz) runny honey

handful of chopped pistachio nuts

1 In a bowl, mix the berries together.

2 Put a layer of the yogurt, a layer of the mixed berries and a squeeze of honey in each glass and repeat until each glass is filled. Top with pistachios and chill until ready to serve.

This is my take on the idea of having a healthy bit of grapefruit to start the day. Baking brings out the flavours and makes the grapefruit very juicy, which wakes the taste buds up for sure! A real pleasure to eat...

HOT BAKED GRAPEFRUIT
WITH CRÈME FRAÎCHE AND HONEY

PREP
10 minutes

COOKING
15 minutes

SERVES 4

2 grapefruits

50ml (2fl oz) medium sherry

4 tbsp demerara sugar

20g (¾oz) butter

4 tbsp crème fraîche

2 tbsp honey

4 sprigs of fresh mint, to decorate

1 Preheat the oven to 200°C/fan 180°C/gas mark 6.

2 Cut the grapefruits in half and loosen the segments by sliding a sharp knife between the peel and the pith, and between each segment, leaving the flesh in the skin. Arrange the 4 grapefruit halves in a roasting tin, cut sides up, then spoon the sherry evenly over each half. Sprinkle generously with demerara sugar and place a small nut of butter on top of each half. Bake in the centre of the oven for 15 minutes.

3 Remove from the oven and spoon over any juices that may remain in the tin. Serve at once, topping each grapefruit half with a tablespoon of crème fraîche and a drizzle of honey to taste. Decorate each with a sprig of mint.

'An apple a day keeps the doctor away'. With this in mind, and not wanting you to smudge your red lipstick, why not try slicing and baking them? Baking intensifies the appley flavour; just adding a little sugar and lemon turns this into a very clean-tasting dish. Think of it as the best bit of an apple pie.

BAKED APPLE SLICES WITH CINNAMON CREAM

PREP
5 minutes

COOKING
20–25 minutes

SERVES 4

4 Braeburns, Coxes or other dessert apples

4 tbsp brown sugar

juice of 1 lemon

1 tbsp ground cinnamon

300ml (10fl oz) whipping cream

1 Preheat the oven to 180°C/fan 160°C/gas mark 4.

2 Core the apples (if using Russet apples, peel them first) and place in a small, shallow ovenproof dish. Sprinkle with the brown sugar, squeeze lemon juice over and bake for 20–25 minutes.

3 Meanwhile, add the cinnamon to the cream and whisk.

4 Serve the apples as soon as they come out of the oven, mixed with a generous dollop of the cinnamon cream for each serving.

CODDLED EGGS

In my early 20s I bought a ceramic pot with a very pretty pattern on it and used it to serve jam. My grandmother thought this was very odd and explained that my jam pot was actually an egg coddler. I now have a variety of egg coddlers and truly don't know what my life would have been like without them. My favourite is an 1871 James Deakin antique egg coddler that sits proudly in my kitchen, looking after the others.

'An egg coddler is a porcelain or pottery cup with a lid that is used to prepare a dish called, appropriately enough, coddled eggs. Coddled eggs are very much like poached eggs, except that the egg is cooked inside the coddler. The egg(s) are broken into the buttered coddler, and seasonings are added, if desired. The coddler is then closed with the lid and partially immersed in boiling water for a few minutes. When the eggs are cooked to the desired firmness, the coddler is lifted from the boiling water, the lid removed, and breakfast is served, in a lovely decorated dish.'

Official quotation from the egg-coddling community.

Scrambled, fried, poached, boiled, or devilled – how do you eat yours? I like to coddle mine.

After you have raided your granny's cupboards and got your hands on an egg coddler, let the coddling begin! Remember one simple rule: 'If it goes with eggs, coddle it.'

CODDLED EGGS: THE BASICS

PREP
5 minutes

COOKING
8 minutes

My favourite fillings:
smoked salmon and chives
baby leaf spinach and truffle oil
pancetta
crumbled feta cheese, a few capers
and a sprig of dill

1 Place the empty coddler(s) in a saucepan and fill the saucepan with cold water until it reaches three-quarters of the way up the side of the coddler(s).

2 Remove the coddler(s) from the saucepan and place the pan of water on the stove over a medium heat. Get your eggs ready while waiting for this to reach boiling point.

3 Butter each coddler and season to taste. Add your chosen filling, an egg, a little more butter and then season again. Screw on the lid and transfer the coddler(s) to the saucepan and boil for 5–7 minutes, depending on the size of the egg(s) and how soft you like the yolk.

4 Either eat the egg(s) from their coddlers with a spoon, or remove them carefully and serve them on pretty plates.

Red is my favourite colour, and I would cook this dish based simply on the visual impact that the juicy ruby tomatoes have on the table. Luckily, they are incredibly tasty, too. At first glance, popping an egg into a tomato may seem a little unusual, but don't knock it till you've tried it.

EGG-STUFFED TOMATOES

PREP
5–10 minutes

COOKING
18–22 minutes

SERVES
Any number – just use one tomato and one egg per person

1 large beefsteak tomato per person

1 tbsp per person of your choice of filling, such as ready-made pesto, grated Cheddar cheese, bacon or pancetta

1 large free-range egg per person

salt and black pepper

1 Preheat the oven to 200°C/fan 180°C/gas mark 6. Lightly oil an ovenproof glass or ceramic dish.

2 With a sharp knife, thinly slice a bit off the bottom of each tomato so that it will sit flat. Cut a lid of about 1cm (½in) from the top of each tomato and set aside. Then, using a small spoon, gently scrape out and discard the pulp and seeds.

3 Put the tomatoes in the prepared dish and spoon in the filling. Crack 1 egg into each tomato and season with salt and pepper, then place the tomato lids back on top.

4 Bake for 18–22 minutes, until the egg whites are set but the yolks are still runny. Serve immediately.

The key to a good frittata is in the beating. Maximum air incorporated into the mixture before baking makes for a very light and fluffy dish. I use shape cutters to cut the frittata into fun or pretty shapes. Embrace the occasion: breakfast for a loved one naturally calls for a heart.

Courgette Frittata

PREP
10 minutes

COOKING
28–30 minutes

SERVES 4

2 tbsp vegetable oil

1 onion, sliced

2 courgettes, finely sliced into half-moon pieces

10 large free-range eggs

salt and black pepper

70g (2½oz) Cheddar cheese, grated

edible gerbera petals, to garnish

1 Preheat the oven to 220°C/fan 200°C/gas mark 7. Line a baking sheet with nonstick baking paper.

2 Heat the oil in a frying pan, add the onion and fry gently for 2 minutes until soft but not coloured. Add the courgette, increase the heat and continue to fry for 4 minutes until golden (you'll get more colour if you don't stir or toss too much). Take off the heat.

3 Beat the eggs in a bowl and season with salt. Stir in the courgette and onion.

4 Transfer the mixture to a 20 × 30cm (8 × 12in) rectangular baking tin and bake for 20 minutes until just set in the centre. Preheat the grill to its highest setting.

5 Sprinkle with cheese and cook under a hot grill for 2 minutes until golden brown and bubbling. Allow to cool slightly.

6 Season with black pepper, then cut into squares or use cutters of your favourite shape. Serve garnished with the edible gerbera petals.

The classic Eggs Benedict consists of a sliced English muffin topped with ham, a poached egg and Hollandaise sauce. Here are some variations: Eggs Florentine swaps ham for spinach; Eggs Montreal swaps ham for salmon; Crab Benedict swaps ham for crab; and Irish Benedict swaps ham for corned beef. This is my take on Eggs Benedict, which includes a quick Hollandaise sauce recipe that is almost foolproof. Eating something with such a smooth, velvety texture is a great start to the day.

Eggs Blackstone

PREP and
COOKING
10–15 minutes
SERVES
6

3 rashers of dry-cured streaky bacon

salt and black pepper

6 slices of ripe tomato

flour, for dredging

6 free-range eggs, poached

about 125ml (4fl oz) Hollandaise sauce

For the Hollandaise sauce

115g (4oz) butter

3 free-range egg yolks

2 tbsp lemon juice

salt and white pepper

PREP
5 minutes

MAKES
250ml
(9fl oz)

1 First make the Hollandaise sauce. Melt the butter in a saucepan over a low heat until it begins to bubble. Remove from the heat and set aside.

2 Put the egg yolks, lemon juice, salt and white pepper in an electric blender. Cover and blend on high speed for about 5 seconds. (You can do this with a hand whisk, but it is much harder work.) Remove the cover and add the melted butter in a slow stream, blending at high speed for about 30 seconds more. The sauce should be smooth with no traces of unincorporated butter. If it's not, replace the cover and continue blending until the butter is completely incorporated, scraping down the sides of the blender if necessary. Transfer to a storage jar.

3 Fry the bacon until crisp. Drain on paper towels and crumble. Season the tomato slices and dredge with flour, then fry in the bacon fat until light golden brown on both sides. Remove and drain on paper towels.

4 Place the tomato slices on a serving platter or individual plates. Sprinkle with the crumbled bacon and place a poached egg on top of each. Serve topped with a generous spoonful of Hollandaise sauce.

Sometimes a recipe develops from having something pretty to cook in and trying to fill it with deliciousness. On my travels, I find many teacups without saucers, and I like to rescue them and give them a home. This simple recipe becomes a talking point at every High Tea. Yes, you can cook things in china; yes, it's like a crème brûlée; and yes, you can use other vegetables when asparagus is not in season!

ASPARAGUS EGG CUSTARDS
WITH PARMESAN WAFERS

PREP
10 minutes
COOKING
34–40 minutes
SERVES 4

200ml (7fl oz) milk

300ml (10fl oz) double cream

1 free-range egg plus 4 free-range egg yolks

salt and black pepper

16 fine asparagus spears

25g (1oz) freshly grated Parmesan cheese

1 Preheat the oven to 170°C/fan 150°C/between gas marks 3 and 4.

2 In a small pan, heat the milk and cream together until almost boiling. Meanwhile, beat the egg and egg yolks together in a bowl and season. Pour the hot milk on to the eggs and mix well. Set aside. Put a kettle on to boil.

3 Cut the asparagus spears in half, reserving the tips. Chop the remainder. Add the chopped asparagus to the egg mixture. Place 4 asparagus tips standing up in each cup, then pour over the egg mixture. Stand the cups in a roasting tin and pour just-boiled water to come halfway up the outside of the dishes. Bake for 30–35 minutes or until just set. Remove the egg custards from the oven and allow to cool for 5 minutes.

4 For the Parmesan wafers, line a baking sheet with nonstick baking paper and sprinkle the cheese into four 6–7cm (2½–2¾in) rounds. Bake for 4–5 minutes or until golden brown – the cheese will spread to make lacy wafers.

5 Serve the egg custards with a Parmesan wafer on top of each cup.

Asparagus Egg Custards with Parmesan Wafers

DR COTTONBOTTOM SHOWS YOU HOW TO MAKE APRONS

Aprons are protective and hygienic items of clothing that are ordinarily worn over the front of the body to stop wear and tear on our clothes. They are also very cute. Here, Dr Cottonbottom shows you how to make our very own Art Deco-inspired Vintage Patisserie aprons.

The Classic Vintage Patisserie Apron

The Pin-up, Pin-on Apron

The Brace-yourself Apron

YOU WILL NEED

1.5m (1¾ yards) of standard-width material ✂ iron ✂ ironing board ✂ pencil ✂ ruler ✂ measuring tape ✂ brown paper or dressmakers' squared pattern paper ✂ scissors ✂ pins ✂ fabric scissors ✂ sewing machine

SEWING LINGO

✂ **Centre front line** – The line in the centre of the pattern that will run straight down the front of your body. If the centre front line of the pattern runs parallel to the selvedge, the pattern is aligned properly.

✂ **Selvedge** – The finished nonfraying edges on a piece of woven fabric that run parallel to the 'warp' of the fabric (up the sides of the piece of material).

✂ **Straight grain** – Runs parallel to the selvedge. When you tug on the straight grain, there is little 'give' in the fabric.

✂ **Cross grain** – Runs perpendicular to the selvedge. When you tug on the cross grain (or bias), the fabric will 'give' a little more than when you tug on the straight grain.

✂ **Backstitch** – A stitch worked in a 'two steps forward, one step back' fashion to ensure the thread is secure and does not unravel.

✂ **Topstitch** – This is most often used on garment edges such as necklines and hems, where it helps facings to stay in place and gives a crisp edge. Decorative topstitching is designed to be visible, and may be done in a fancy thread or with a special type of stitch.

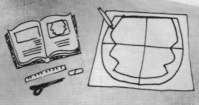

STEP 1 Prepare the material by washing it at the appropriate setting, then leaving it to dry. Once it is dry, give it a good iron to get all the creases out.

STEP 2 Create a pattern for your chosen apron on brown paper or dressmakers' squared pattern paper using the measurements given on pages 50–51.

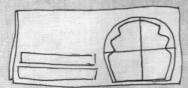

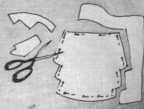

STEP 3 Fold your material in half lengthways and lay your pattern out on to it, making sure that the centre front line is parallel to the straight grain. If the material has a printed pattern, however, the centre front line should be parallel to the cross grain, which runs perpendicular to the selvedge.

STEP 4 Once you are happy with it, pin the pattern down and cut it using fabric scissors to ensure a clean line. Remove the pattern.

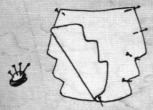

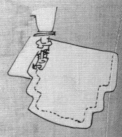

STEP 5 You should have two apron pieces and four belt pieces (and four braces pieces if you're making the Brace-yourself Apron). Place the pieces right-sides together, and pin.

STEP 6 Leaving the top open on the main apron and the belt, use backstitch to stitch around the edges of each piece, with a 1.5cm (⅝in) seam allowance.

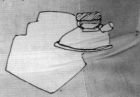

STEP 7 Clip 'Vs' into the seam allowance at the corners and trim excess material away from the straight edges. Clip 'Vs' along the curved edge to ease the bulk when the apron is turned inside out.

STEP 8 Iron the seams open, then turn the apron right-side out and iron flat. Repeat steps 7 and 8 for the belt (and the braces if you're making the Brace-yourself Apron).

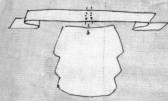

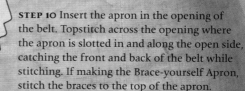

STEP 9 Overlap and stitch together the ends of the two belt pieces. Align the apron's centre point with the centre point of the belt.

STEP 10 Insert the apron in the opening of the belt. Topstitch across the opening where the apron is slotted in and along the open side, catching the front and back of the belt while stitching. If making the Brace-yourself Apron, stitch the braces to the top of the apron.

The Classic Vintage Patisserie Apron

107cm (42in)

10cm (4in) | x4 | 8cm (3¼in)

100cm (39½in)

34cm (13½in)

37cm (14½in) | x2 | 23.5cm (9¼in)

9cm (3½in)

4cm (1½in)

The Pin-up, Pin-on Apron

107cm (42in)

10cm (4in) | x4 | 8cm (3¼in)

100cm (39½in)

20.5cm (8¼in)

32cm (12½in)

29cm (11½in)

x2

18cm (7in)

28cm (11in)

28cm (11in)

21cm (8¼in)

x2

43cm (17in) | 34cm (13½in)

40cm (16in)

The Brace-yourself Apron

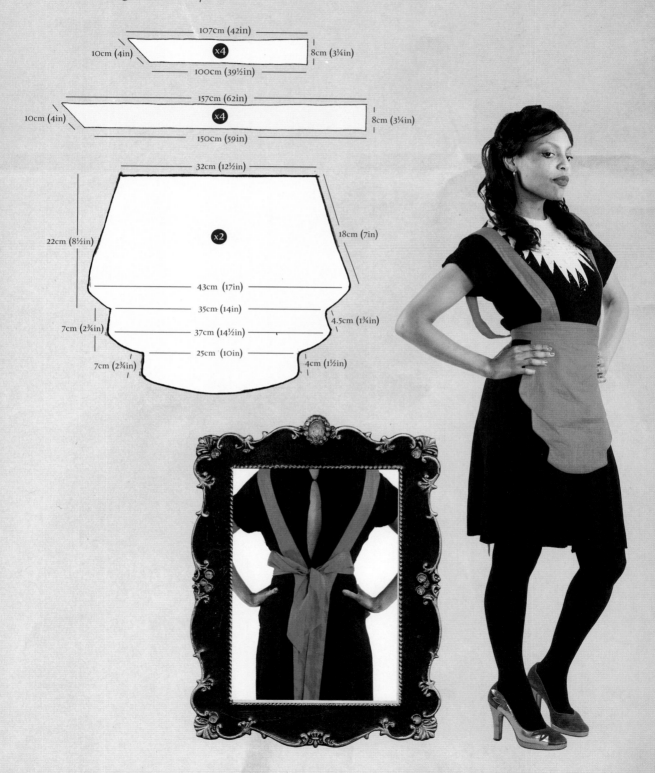

107cm (42in)

x4

10cm (4in) 8cm (3¼in)

100cm (39½in)

157cm (62in)

x4

10cm (4in) 8cm (3¼in)

150cm (59in)

32cm (12½in)

x2

22cm (8½in) 18cm (7in)

43cm (17in)

35cm (14in)

7cm (2¾in) 37cm (14½in) 4.5cm (1¾in)

25cm (10in)

7cm (2¾in) 4cm (1½in)

These dainty soufflés look gorgeous baked in fine china teacups. Take care when separating the eggs, as even a trace of yolk will stop the whites rising. Use a clean, dry bowl and beaters, as any residue will prevent the whites forming a firm peak. After putting the mixture in the cups, wipe around the insides of the rims; this allows the soufflés to rise uniformly. Finally, resist all urges to open the oven door before the cooking time is up!

SMOKED SALMON soufflé

PREP
25–35 minutes

COOKING
10 minutes

SERVES 8

50g (1¾oz) butter,
plus extra for greasing
50g (1¾oz) plain flour
300ml (½ pint) milk
3 free-range eggs, separated
salt and pepper
100g (3½oz) smoked salmon, chopped

1 Preheat the oven to 200°C/fan 180°C/gas mark 6. Lightly grease 8 small teacups or ramekins.

2 Melt the butter in a pan over a low heat. Add the flour and cook for a minute, stirring all the time. Remove from the heat and gradually add the milk, whisking continuously. (If you don't use a whisk, there may be lumps in the sauce; if so, just pass the mixture through a sieve.) When all the milk has been incorporated, return the mixture to the heat and stir until thickened, then remove from the heat again and allow to cool.

3 Beat the egg yolks and season. When the sauce is cool enough to dip your finger in it, beat in the yolks. Then mix the smoked salmon into the sauce.

4 Using a clean, dry bowl, whisk the egg whites until so stiff that, when you turn the bowl upside-down, none of the mixture spills out. Very gently fold this into the smoked salmon mixture.

5 Nudge the mixture carefully into the prepared teacups or ramekins. Smooth the tops and wipe inside each rim. Bake for 10 minutes, until risen and golden. These airy bites of deliciousness are best served immediately.

Fishcakes are in my top 5 nostalgic foods. When my mum made them, I stood in the kitchen as they came out of the fryer, waiting for them to cool. She used salmon, but you can use any fish, even a mixture. Smoked haddock is my favourite. Buy 'boneless' fish, and run your fingers over it to check for any remaining bones.

HADDOCK AND POTATO MINI CAKES

PREP
40 minutes

COOKING
20–25 minutes

SERVES 4

600ml (1 pint) semi-skimmed milk
½ onion, peeled but not chopped
1 bay leaf
225g (8oz) smoked haddock, preferably undyed
225g (8oz) potatoes, unpeeled
25g (1oz) Parmesan cheese, grated
salt and black pepper
1 free-range egg
a little plain flour
100g (3½oz) fresh white breadcrumbs
vegetable oil, for deep-frying

1 Heat 500ml (18fl oz) of milk in a pan with the onion and bay leaf until it simmers. Remove from the heat and leave to infuse for 15 minutes. Return to the heat and, when it is simmering, add the fish. Simmer for 7 minutes. Remove the fish from the milk, set aside to cool, then flake into small pieces.

2 Boil the potatoes in the milk until they are cooked (about 10–15 minutes). You may need to add a little more milk. Drain the potatoes and remove the bay leaf. Mash the potatoes with the Parmesan, salt and pepper. When the mixture is creamy, fold in the flaked haddock and shape into 8 cakes.

3 Beat the egg with the remaining milk in a bowl. Put some flour in a second bowl and the breadcrumbs in a third. Dip each cake into the flour, then into the egg–milk mixture, and finally into the breadcrumbs.

4 Preheat 8cm (3¼in) of oil to 160–180°C in a large heavy-based saucepan (you'll need a cooking thermometer) or electric deep-fat fryer and fry a few cakes at a time for 2–3 minutes, turning them with a slotted spoon as they are cooking, until they are golden. Drain on kitchen paper and serve warm.

I sometimes feel like donning tartan when I prepare this recipe. The oatcakes are a perfect accompaniment to the buttery pâté and the whisky marmalade adds an extra zing to this Scottish-themed dish. Seek out triangular oatcakes at the bigger supermarkets or small independent delis. It is worth the extra effort as it makes the dish look a bit more interesting and is also easier to eat (try it if you don't believe me).

KIPPER Pâté on oatcakes with Whisky Marmalade

PREP
20–25 minutes
SERVES 8

300g (10½oz) cooked kipper fillet or boil-in-the-bag kippers

100g (3½oz) butter, at room temperature

2 tsp dry sherry

freshly ground black pepper

1 tsp chopped tarragon

½ tsp ground mace

16 oatcakes

240g (8½oz) Whisky Marmalade (*see* page 85)

100ml (3½fl oz) crème fraîche

sprigs of tarragon, to garnish

1 Remove the skin from the cooked kipper and flake the meat into a bowl.

2 Melt the butter in a pan and use a large spoon to skim off the white solids on the surface. Discard these. Pour the 'clarified' butter over the kipper flesh, then add the sherry, pepper, tarragon and mace and mix everything together with a fork until it reaches a coarse, textured consistency. Alternatively, blitz with a food processor for about 30 seconds until everything is well combined. Chill in the refrigerator until needed.

3 To serve, place 2 oatcakes per person on a plate and spread generously with the Whisky Marmalade. Pile a heaped teaspoon of kipper pâté on top and finish with a dollop of crème fraîche. Garnish with sprigs of tarragon.

I never used to be a black pudding fan and always turned up my nose when offered some. That was probably quite unfair, as I had never even sampled it. Then one day, on the insistence of a friend, I tried it, and it tasted fabulous – like a spicy sausage, but grainier. From then on I was a convert, and looked at ways of incorporating it into my cooking. It pairs superbly with scallops both in taste and texture – the crispy, salty bites of the pudding really complement the sweet silkiness of the scallops. If you have a friend who is averse to black pudding, let them try it this way – I'm sure they will be surprised at how good it tastes.

KING SCALLOPS WITH CRISPY BLACK PUDDING

12 king scallops, in the shell
4 slices of black pudding
extra-virgin olive oil
sea salt and black pepper

PREP
15 minutes
COOKING
4–5 minutes
SERVES 4

1 Remove the scallops from their shells and reserve the shells for serving. Trim away the tough muscle from the scallop, leaving the pink coral attached.

2 Dice the black pudding and pan-fry it in a little olive oil until it is crispy (about 2 minutes). Set aside.

3 Coat the scallops very lightly with olive oil, then season. Heat a dry frying pan until very hot. Add the scallops and cook for 1 minute, turn over and cook for 1 minute more, until they are sealed and caramelized. Divide the scallops between the 4 shells and sprinkle with the black pudding. Serve immediately.

Many (like myself) would associate the sausage roll with our parents' cocktail parties, or view it as a sinful piece of convenience food. However, prepared with fresh ingredients, and with a little twist and shake, your average roll is transformed not only into a hair accessory and binoculars, but also a scrumptious bite-sized delight! I prefer chicken in the morning, but feel free to use this recipe with other meats, even sausage.

CHICKEN AND BACON ROLLS

PREP
20 minutes

COOKING
20 minutes

MAKES
24 rolls

2 boneless, skinless chicken breasts, chopped into small pieces

1 garlic clove, crushed

2 free-range eggs, beaten separately

1 tbsp double cream

230g pack (2 rolls) of ready-rolled puff pastry

plain flour, for dusting

8 rashers of thin streaky bacon

large bunch of basil

25g (1oz) sesame seeds

1 Whizz the chicken and garlic in a processor until the chicken is minced, then add one of the beaten eggs and the cream. Set aside.

2 Lay 1 piece of pastry on a lightly floured surface. Arrange half the bacon rashers over it, leaving a 15mm (⅝in) margin at the top and bottom edges of the pastry rectangle. Cover with half the basil leaves. Now spread half the chicken mixture in a long sausage shape alongside the bottom margin. Brush the top margin with a little of the remaining beaten egg, then roll the bottom margin over the chicken mixture and roll up the pastry tightly. Press down the top margin to seal. Repeat with the other piece of pastry and the remaining filling. Wrap in the pastry's original paper or in clingfilm and chill for 10 minutes in the refrigerator. Preheat the oven to 200°C/180°C fan/gas mark 6.

3 Remove the rolls from the refrigerator and unwrap. Cut each one into 12 pieces. Place on 2 baking sheets that have been lined with nonstick baking paper. Brush with the remaining egg, then sprinkle with sesame seeds. Bake for 20 minutes until golden.

This is a lovely mixture of soft potatoes and crispy bacon that can be either griddled or fried. It's a fabulous accompaniment to all the other savoury dishes, and can be prepared in advance and left in the refrigerator until guests arrive.

POTATO AND BACON PANCAKES

PREP
20 minutes

COOKING
6 minutes

SERVES 4

6 slices of crispy streaky bacon or pancetta

300g (10½oz) cooked mashed potatoes (when drained, leave for 5 minutes to 'dry' before mashing)

4 spring onions, sliced

2 tbsp flour

bacon fat, for frying (optional)

1 Crumble the crispy bacon or pancetta into a bowl and then add the potato, spring onion and 1 tablespoon of the flour. Mix well.

2 Dust your hands with the remaining flour and form the mixture into 12 balls, each about the size of a plum, then flatten into circles that are about 5mm (¼in) thick.

3 Either griddle the pancakes in a dry, nonstick pan or fry them in bacon fat for 3 minutes each side or until golden brown.

I have a love-hate relationship with quails' eggs: I really like to eat them but I hate to peel them! Yet, teamed with Scotch eggs, these little delicacies are to die for. The lemon cuts through the meat, making this a really light dish and simply delicious. My top tip for peeling quails' eggs is: after boiling, soak them in vinegar for 12 hours. The shell should disintegrate, leaving just the membrane to peel.

PORK AND LEMON QUAIL SCOTCH EGGS

PREP
25–30 minutes

COOKING
10–15 minutes

SERVES
4–6

350g (12oz) good-quality sausagemeat or chipolatas with skin removed

grated rind of 1 lemon

small bunch of thyme

12 quails' eggs

a little plain flour

1 free-range egg, well beaten

400g (14oz) fine homemade breadcrumbs

sunflower oil, for deep-frying

1 Put the sausagemeat or chipolatas in a bowl with the lemon rind. Pluck the leaves off the thyme and add to the bowl. Mix well with your hands.

2 Place the eggs in a saucepan of cold water and bring to a gentle simmer. Simmer for 3 minutes. Run the eggs under cold water for 3 minutes, then shell and roll in a little flour. Take a heaped tablespoon of the sausagemeat mixture, put it in the palm of your hand, flatten it, then curl it up to make a little bowl. Put a floured egg in the hollow and carefully mould the sausagemeat all around it. Roll in flour, coat with beaten egg and cover with breadcrumbs. Repeat until all the sausage mixture is used up.

3 Preheat about 8cm (3¼in) of oil to 160–180°C in a large heavy-based saucepan (you'll need a cooking thermometer) or electric deep-fat fryer and fry the Scotch eggs a few at a time for 2–3 minutes, turning them as they are cooking, until they are golden; then use a slotted spoon to transfer them on to kitchen paper to drain. Serve immediately.

Devilled kidneys tend to have a little bite, so I relish the idea of keeping them caged. This is a classic recipe, but the bread lattice gives this dish crunch, texture, a buttery taste and STYLE!

CAGED DEVILLED KIDNEYS

PREP
20 minutes

COOKING
15 minutes

SERVES 2

100g (3½oz) butter

2 slices of white bread

6 lambs' kidneys, trimmed and quartered

good pinch of cayenne pepper

2 tsp Worcestershire sauce

½ tsp mustard powder

1 tbsp lemon juice

1 tbsp chopped parsley

1 Preheat the oven to 180°C/fan 160°C/gas mark 4. Melt a quarter of the butter. Brush the outsides of 2 teacups or dariole moulds with this, then place them upside-down on a baking sheet.

2 To make the cages, trim the crusts from the bread and roll the trimmed bread flat with a rolling pin. Butter both sides of the bread with half the remaining butter. Cut into 5mm (¼in) strips. Weave the strips into 2 lattice shapes and roll them again. Carefully place the lattices on top of the upside-down prepared teacups or dariole moulds. Bake for 7 minutes, or until golden brown. Remove from the oven and allow to cool for 5 minutes.

3 Heat a dry frying pan, then add the remaining butter. When it has melted, add the kidneys and toss to cook evenly. Once the kidneys have coloured, add the cayenne pepper, Worcestershire sauce, mustard powder and lemon juice, stirring for a further 2 minutes to coat the kidneys thoroughly. Stir in the parsley.

4 To serve, divide the kidneys between 2 plates and then carefully arrange a cage over the top of each serving.

HOW TO DECORATE CHINA

I've often compared buying china to buying a dress. Sometimes I like the shape of the dress and sometimes I like the pattern of the fabric. Luckily, when I've found that perfect dress shape and not liked the pattern I've dyed it. But for quite some time I didn't know there was a ceramic paint available for china that would set in a domestic oven. Genius and life-changing? Nearly. So next time you are in a charity shop or raiding your granny's cupboard, don't be put off by an uninviting china pattern. Get your brushes out and be creative!

YOU WILL NEED

newspaper ✂ old china ✂ cleaning cloth ✂ ceramic paints (in a range of colours, including white; metallics work especially well) ✂ plastic gloves ✂ paint sponges or brushes (in varying thicknesses) ✂ masking tape ✂ scissors

STEP 1 Lay out newspaper on a clean, dry surface so that you have a good-sized work area and won't ruin any furniture. Clean your china, using a cloth, to remove any dust or dirt.

STEP 2 Begin by whitewashing each piece using white ceramic paint and a sponge. You may find it easier to wear plastic gloves and hold the china while painting so that you can ensure an even coverage. Don't be tempted to apply the paint too thickly as it will clot and drip when drying. Sponges work better than brushes because they will not leave streak marks.

STEP 3 Apply a second layer of whitewash if needed in order to block out any pattern on the china. Wait for the pieces to dry thoroughly before continuing; this can vary, but takes approximately 20 minutes. If you whitewash all the pieces together, you can start the next stage with your first piece while waiting for the others to dry.

STEP 4 Choose a design. This could be stripes, checks or freehand. Consider your colours carefully – you may only want to use one colour over the whitewash or a few more.

STEP 5 Using masking tape, block out any areas that you don't want to be exposed when painting the second colour. If you cut skinny strips of tape, the scissors may leave wobbly edges which will create an uneven paint line. In this case, use the outside edges of the tape and overlap two strips to form one final strip so the edges will be clean. It is important to ensure the white paint layer is completely dry before using masking tape, or the white will be lifted when you attempt to remove it later. When ready to paint, use a sponge for large sections, and a thin paintbrush to fill in smaller areas.

STEP 6 When this layer is dry, carefully peel off the masking tape. If lots of paint has dried on top of the tape it can leave a strange peeled-off section attached to the china. You can either try to trim the excess, or fold it back on itself on to the coordinating colour, so that it will not be visible.

STEP 7 To seal your paintwork, preheat your kitchen oven to 180°C/160°C fan/gas mark 4 and bake the painted china for 45 minutes, but keep an eye on it after 30 minutes and remove if the colours start darkening.

Baked Brie is a gooey delight. The textures of the cheese, almonds and puff pastry all combine to make each mouthful positively sinful and wickedly delicious.

BaKeD BRie IN PUFF PaSTRy

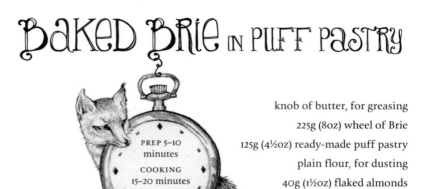

PREP 5–10 minutes

COOKING 15–20 minutes

SERVES 8

knob of butter, for greasing
225g (8oz) wheel of Brie
125g (4½oz) ready-made puff pastry
plain flour, for dusting
40g (1½oz) flaked almonds

1 Preheat the oven to 180°C/fan 160°C/gas mark 4. Lightly grease a 23cm (9in) pie dish.

2 Slice the wheel of Brie in half horizontally, to give 2 thinner wheels.

3 Using a rolling pin, roll out the puff pastry on a lightly floured surface to a thickness of 5mm (¼in), then lay this in the pie dish. Place half of the Brie rind-side down on top of it and sprinkle almonds evenly over the top. Place the other half of the Brie (rind-side up) over the almonds. Pull the edges of the pastry dough around the Brie to cover and seal with a little water.

4 Bake for 15–20 minutes. Allow to cool for 5 minutes before serving.

When a good friend told me you could make pancakes from cottage cheese, I just had to pop to the shop immediately to buy a pot and test. Who would have thought that this ugly, tasteless cheese could make something rather yummy? This is a dish I always get my friends to try before I reveal the main ingredient.

cottage cheese pancakes

PREP
10 minutes

COOKING
10–20 minutes

MAKES 20 small
pancakes

3 large free-range eggs, separated

225g (8oz) cottage cheese

25g (1oz) caster sugar

35g (1¼oz) plain flour

½ tsp baking powder

¼ tsp ground cinnamon

pinch of salt

knob of butter or some cooking spray, for greasing

grated rind of 1 lemon, plus 1 lemon, cut into wedges

icing sugar, for dusting

1 Beat the egg yolks lightly. In a separate bowl beat the egg whites until stiff, glossy peaks form.

2 Stir the egg yolks, cottage cheese, sugar, flour, baking powder, cinnamon and salt together in a medium-sized bowl. Whisk in one-third of the egg whites then, with a spatula, gently fold in the rest.

3 Grease a griddle with cooking spray or butter, then heat over a medium–high heat – the griddle is ready when a drop of batter sizzles on contact. Cook the pancakes in batches. Spoon about 4 tablespoons of batter per pancake on to the griddle. Cook each pancake until the surface bubbles and the edges are slightly dry (this takes only about 1 minute). Flip the pancakes and continue cooking until the undersides are golden brown (about 3 more minutes). Remove and keep warm. Repeat until all the batter is used up.

4 Serve the pancakes sprinkled with grated lemon rind and icing sugar, with lemon wedges on the side.

Funnily enough, potatoes and flowers are two things that always make me smile. In this recipe, the delicate potatoes are cooked in butter, so all their starches are preserved. Because of the no-water element, the finished Onion and Potato Flowers are sticky and slightly gluey – delightful!

ONION and POTATO FLOWERS

PREP
25 minutes

COOKING
55–60 minutes

SERVES 4

100g (3½oz) butter, melted and warm
500g (1lb 2oz) onions, sliced
salt and black pepper
2 sprigs of rosemary, plus extra to garnish
400g (14oz) Desiree or Maris Piper potatoes

1 Line 4 individual tartlet tins with removable bases, each about 5cm (2in) in diameter, or 1 larger ovenproof dish, with nonstick baking paper. Preheat the oven to 190°C/fan 170°C/gas mark 5.

2 Heat about a quarter of the butter in a large pan over a medium heat. Add the onion, a little salt and the rosemary sprigs. Reduce the heat, cover and sweat the onion for about 20 minutes. Remove the rosemary and set aside.

3 Peel the potatoes and immediately cut into wafer-thin slices directly into a bowl containing the rest of the warm butter. The thinner the slices, the better the dish will be. Don't wash the potato once sliced, as you want the starch to stick the slices together. Season with salt and pepper.

4 Start to layer the potato neatly into the prepared tins or dish, overlapping the slices slightly to give a flower effect. When you have piled in half the potato, add the onion, then continue layering the potato until it is all used.

5 Bake for 35–40 minutes until the potato is soft. Remove from the oven and leave the flowers to rest in the tins or dish for 10 minutes before removing. Serve garnished with rosemary sprigs.

The more exotic the mixture of fungi you use for this, the more interesting the final dish. Add cream and a touch of tarragon at the end of cooking and you'll have 'fancy mushrooms on toast'. I serve it on homemade melba toast, which is easy to make, so no excuses. This dish is so delicious there won't be 'mushroom' for anything else. (I blame my father for my bad jokes.)

MUSHROOMS ON HOMEMADE MELBA TOAST

PREP
5–10 minutes

COOKING
5–6 minutes

SERVES 4

oil for frying

4 large handfuls of mixed fungi, such as oyster, shiitake, chestnut and button mushrooms

1 garlic clove

knob of butter

4 tbsp double cream

small pack of tarragon, chopped

4 slices of white bread

edible carnation petals, to garnish

1 Heat a dry frying pan, then add a little oil. Cook the fungi and garlic clove for 1–2 minutes, toss, and cook for another minute. Add the butter, toss, remove the garlic clove, then add the cream and tarragon and mix well. Take off the heat and set aside.

2 Preheat the grill to its highest setting. For the Melba toast, toast the bread, remove the crusts and, using a shape cutter, cut into any shape you like. Cut each slice of toast in half horizontally to make 2 thinner slices. Put under a hot grill for a few minutes, turning once, until they are brown and crisp.

3 Layer the mushrooms on top of the toast as soon as the toast is ready, and serve garnished with edible carnation petals.

I have always wondered where the 'rabbit' is in a rarebit... The slightly lemony flavour of the soft Welsh goats' cheese in this version goes really well with the leeks.

leek and goats' cheese rarebit with chive grass

PREP
10 minutes

COOKING
12–15 minutes

SERVES 4

1 ciabatta loaf

50g (1¾oz) butter

2 leeks, finely shredded

25g (1oz) plain flour

1 tsp mustard powder

150ml (5fl oz) milk

115g (4oz) creamy Welsh goats' cheese

salt and black pepper

small bunch of chives, chopped, to garnish

1 Preheat the oven to 180°C/160°C fan/gas mark 4. Cut the ciabatta into 2cm (¾in) thick slices and place in the oven for 5–8 minutes until crisp and golden. Rest on a wire rack to keep crisp while you prepare the rarebit.

2 Melt the butter in a medium-sized pan and gently sweat the leek for 2–3 minutes so that it softens but doesn't brown. Stir in the flour and mustard powder. Gradually stir in the milk and bring to simmering point to make a thick sauce.

3 Now stir in the goats' cheese and cook gently until melted. Season well. Preheat the grill to its highest setting.

4 Spoon the rarebit generously on to the toasted ciabatta. Brown under the grill for 2 minutes until bubbling and serve immediately, garnished with chopped chives.

FLOWER ARRANGING

On Sundays I like to visit my local flower market. It's in a residential part of town, and as I approach the only clues that it's taking place are the people walking down the quiet roads nearby hiding behind towers of flowers.

By this point my heart is already pounding with excitement. As I turn the corner to enter the market, it feels like I've been magically transported to a 'flower Narnia'. There are such delights for my eyes and nose. Often the flowers I buy are for gifts, and sometimes they are a gift for me. I get joy from both.

Flowers feature at every event I host. Tea parties must excite all the senses, so do be creative. Any vessel can be used to display flowers. I use teapots that have lost their lids, milk jugs, sugar bowls... even chandeliers!

If you want to take your flower arranging one step further, ask your florist for some green floral foam to support your flowers. This allows you to place the flowers accurately. You can then water the foam to keep them fresh. However you decide to play in flower Narnia, enjoy. Here are my monthly picks to get your creativity flowing.

 June: Rose June marks the start of the tea-party season and is also the month of the rose, the most symbolic of all flowers. Synonymous with romance, roses speak of a bygone era. Vintage varieties are the Tea Rose and the sweet-smelling Damask Rose, which will fill your home with its wonderful scent. Both are full-budded, so why not place single blooms in vintage teacups and dot them around your home? Alternatively, dry them and scatter their petals around your table.

 July: Larkspur Blue or deep violet in colour and beautiful.

 August: Poppy Dramatic, fiery and passionate in appearance.

 September: Aster The name of this flower is derived from the Ancient Greek word meaning 'star', due to the star shape that its petals make.

 October: Calendula More commonly known as pot marigold, calendula flowers vary in colour, from pale yellow to orangey red.

 November: Chrysanthemum These large blooms often have bold pink petals. Tie them together with a satin ribbon and display them in a vintage birdcage, or arrange the flowers in vintage teapots.

 December: Dahlia Black Narcissus With its dark red, cactus-style blooms, these unusual flowers are dramatic and beautiful. Holly and mistletoe are also winter favourites.

 January: Snowdrop So sweet and elegant, these delicate flowers have a wintry feel about them. Beautiful displayed in vintage glasses.

 February: Violet Simply gorgeous, violet in colour and often with heart-shaped petals – perfect for your Valentine.

 March: Jonquil Extremely fragrant and fresh for spring.

 April: Sweet Pea These bright, highly scented flowers come in a variety of pink, purple and white shades and have been cultivated since the 17th century.

 May: Lily-of-the-Valley This flower's name suggests a lady-like glamour. Put these bell-shaped beauties into a teapot and let them pour over on to the table.

This is a favourite breakfast of mine. I love the combination of hazelnut chocolate spread and sweet, buttery brioche; it's like a rich, chocolatey version of eggy bread. Make sure you fry it for long enough so that its crispy and brown; the sweet golden burnt bits of the brioche are the best.

Toasted Chocolate Hearts

PREP
10 minutes

COOKING
8–10 minutes

MAKES 6

1 brioche loaf
6 tbsp hazelnut chocolate spread
1 free-range egg, beaten
10g (¼oz) butter

1 Cut 12 slices of brioche, each about 1cm (½in) thick.

2 Spread 6 slices with a tablespoon of hazelnut chocolate spread each. Place the other 6 slices on top to make sandwiches. Cut into heart shapes with a shape cutter.

3 Coat each sandwich with a little beaten egg. Melt the butter in a frying pan and fry the sandwiches on a medium heat until golden brown on both sides. Serve immediately.

A tea loaf is a light, tasty, traditional English cake that has been sweetened with natural fruits, spices and often honey. This is quite a healthy recipe as there is very little fat, and the sweetness comes from honey and the plums (flavours that go beautifully together). It's also easy to make as there is no furious beating – just a few stirs with a wooden spoon and you're done. Serve warm, as it is, or slathered with butter (which then mitigates the healthiness!). I like mine toasted, with a big mug of tea.

PLUM AND HONEY TEA BREAD

PREP
10–15 minutes

COOKING
50–55 minutes

MAKES
a 450g (1lb) loaf

200g (7oz) plain flour

1 tsp baking powder

1 tsp bicarbonate of soda

1 tsp ground cinnamon

¼ tsp ground nutmeg

½ tsp salt

175ml (6fl oz) buttermilk or low-fat yogurt

125ml (4fl oz) honey

2 tbsp vegetable oil

1 free-range egg, beaten

3 plums, stoned and chopped

60g (2¼oz) walnuts, chopped

1 Preheat the oven to 160°C/fan 140°C/gas mark 3. Grease a 450g (1lb) loaf tin. Sift the flour, baking powder, bicarbonate of soda, spices and salt into a large bowl and mix well.

2 Put the buttermilk or yogurt, honey, oil and egg in a separate bowl and mix until combined. Stir the buttermilk or yogurt mixture into the dry ingredients, then fold in the plums and walnuts.

3 Pour into the prepared loaf tin. The mixture should not fill the tin – leave a gap of about 3cm (1¼in) at the top. Bake for 50–55 minutes or until a wooden pick inserted near the centre comes out clean. Allow to cool a little in the tin and serve while still warm.

Quick Strawberry Jam

Whisky Marmalade

Orange and Lemon Curd

BREAD and JAM

Making jam is wonderful: the smell of fruit and sugar wafting through a slightly steamy kitchen transports me back to my granny's house where I would stand on a chair, slowly stirring a big pot of it. If you've never made jam, you're going to be surprised at how easy it is. The important thing is to make sure everything you use is spotlessly clean, otherwise the jam will spoil. To me, the best thing about making your own jam is that you can experiment with all sorts of exciting flavour combinations – kiwi fruit and pineapple, anyone?

This is a really easy recipe and perfect for all you novice jam-makers. The lemon juice is used not just for taste, but also to help the jam set, as strawberries are low in pectin (a natural setting agent). To make the best-tasting jam, choose a strawberry variety that is very sweet and flavoursome.

QUICK STRAWBERRY JAM

PREP
35 minutes
COOKING
1 hour
MAKES 2 × 375g
(13oz) jars

400g (14oz) strawberries, halved

450g (1lb) caster sugar

4 tsp fresh lemon juice

1 Before you start, sterilize 2 jam jars by washing them thoroughly in hot soapy water and rinsing in warm water. Preheat the oven to 140°C/fan 120°C/gas mark 1, and stand the jars upside-down on a rack in the oven to dry for about 30 minutes. Alternatively, after rinsing, dry the jars in the microwave for 1 minute – they must be wet, but not filled with water or they will explode.

2 Combine the strawberries and sugar in a medium-sized saucepan and bring them to a simmer over a medium–high heat, stirring frequently. Reduce the heat to medium and continue to simmer for 1 hour or until thick, stirring occasionally. Remove from the heat and stir in the lemon juice.

3 Pour into the warm jars, seal and allow to cool. Store in the refrigerator. The jam will keep for 6 months.

The creamy, sweet-sharp taste of lemon curd is gorgeous, but the addition of oranges here curbs the tang and adds more depth and dimension to the flavour. This luminous sunshine-yellow curd is very versatile. It's fabulous spread on buttery toast, but works equally well as a filling for a deep dark chocolate sponge (add a bit of cream just to lighten it a little); drizzled over crushed meringues, strawberries and yogurt for a quick dessert; or spooned generously over the top of a cheesecake. My all-time favourite is dolloping it on some pancakes strewn with blueberries and raspberries – heaven!

ORANGE AND LEMON CURD

PREP
35 minutes
COOKING
15–20 minutes
MAKES 2 × 375g
(13oz) jars

125g (4½oz) butter

250g (9oz) caster sugar

grated rind and juice of
2 lemons and 2 oranges

4 large free-range eggs, beaten

1 Before you start, sterilize 2 jam jars by following the instructions to the left.

2 Cut the butter into small pieces and put it into a heavy-based saucepan with the sugar and the orange and lemon juice and rind. Heat gently, stirring, until the sugar has dissolved. Add the beaten eggs and keep stirring for 5–10 minutes until the mixture thickens.

3 Pour the curd into the warm jars, seal and allow to cool. Store in the refrigerator, ready for breakfast. The curd will keep for 6 months.

This full-bodied marmalade is excellent with savoury dishes such as the kipper pâté on page 56, or a ploughman's lunch. I like it on a sharp cheese sandwich, too. You can also stir it into a Victoria sponge mixture for a delectably moist orange cake.

WHISKY MARMALADE

PREP
35 minutes

COOKING
25–30 minutes

MAKES 4kg (9lb)
6 small jars

850g can prepared thin-cut Seville oranges

150ml (5fl oz) whisky

1.8kg (4lb) caster sugar

10g (¼oz) butter

1 Before you start, sterilize 6 small jam jars by following the instructions on the opposite page.

2 Empty the oranges into a large (4.5 litre/8 pint) saucepan over a medium heat. Add 425ml (15fl oz) water (if the orange can has a measure mark, you can use this – it is halfway up), then add the whisky.

3 Stir in the sugar and bring to the boil, stirring continuously with a wooden spoon. Reduce the heat and keep on the boil for a further 15 minutes, stirring occasionally. Add a little butter if needed to disperse any foam.

4 Remove from the heat. Test the marmalade by spooning ½ teaspoon on to a cold saucer and leaving it in a cool place for 2 minutes. Run your finger over the surface – the marmalade should wrinkle. If it doesn't, boil the contents of the pan for another few minutes and test again.

5 Stand the marmalade for a further 2–3 minutes before pouring into the warm jars. Stir well to disperse the peel. Seal each jar and allow to cool. The marmalade will keep for 6 months.

BAKING BREAD

Baking bread or eating it – which is more satisfying? I can never quite decide. Doing both is an overload of pleasure and, when you have got the knack, the possibilities are endless. Fresh warm bread is a delight with my Savoury Creams and Butters (*see page 120*), and you can also make tiny rolls to fit with the delicate tea-party feel.

HERBY WHITE ROLLS

PREP
15 minutes plus 30 minutes proving

COOKING
30 minutes

MAKES 12 rolls

1kg (2lb 4oz) strong white flour, plus extra for dusting

600ml (1 pint) warm water

30g (1oz) fresh yeast

3 tbsp olive oil or rapeseed oil, plus extra for greasing and spraying

20g (¾oz) salt

handful of mixed fresh herbs, such as sage, rosemary and thyme, chopped

caraway, poppy, pumpkin or sesame seeds, to decorate (optional)

1 Mix together the flour, water, yeast and oil in a bowl. Turn on to a floured work surface, flatten, then knead well for 10 minutes and flatten again. Sprinkle the salt and herbs over the dough. Knead the dough for a further 5 minutes, then form into a ball.

2 Grease a large bowl with a little oil, put the dough in it and spray with a little more oil. Cover the bowl with a warm, damp tea towel and leave the dough to prove for 10 minutes. ('Proving' means letting the bread relax, to give the yeast time to react and make the dough rise.)

3 Turn the dough on to a floured work surface and pull off pieces to make 12 rolls. Sprinkle them with flour, or wet them and sprinkle with your chosen seeds, if liked, and leave them to rise for a further 20 minutes. Preheat the oven to 200°C/fan 180°C/gas mark 6.

4 Bake the rolls for about 30 minutes, until golden.

Irish Soda Bread is great if you want to make a quick bread in under an hour. It's very simple to make as you don't need to wait for the dough to rise, and it's delicious eaten hot out of the oven with butter and jam.

IRISH SODA BREAD

PREP
10 minutes

COOKING
40–45 minutes

SERVES
4–6

175g (6oz) self-raising wholemeal flour

175g (6oz) plain flour, plus extra for dusting

½ tsp bicarbonate of soda

½ tsp salt

300ml (½ pint) buttermilk

1 Preheat the oven to 200°C/fan 180°C/gas mark 6.

2 Sift both types of flour, the bicarbonate of soda and salt into a mixing bowl. Make a well in the centre and pour in the buttermilk, stirring as you go, until the mixture forms a tough dough. Add a little more milk if the mixture is not coming together.

3 Turn on to a floured work surface, knead lightly for about a minute, then shape into a round.

4 Put the round of dough on a lightly floured baking sheet and dust with flour. Mark a deep cross with the handle of a wooden spoon, pushing two-thirds of the way through the loaf. Bake for 40–45 minutes, until the loaf sounds hollow when tapped underneath.

5 Cool on a wire rack if you like a crunchy crust, or wrapped in a clean tea towel if you prefer a soft crust.

I prefer savoury muffins to sweet ones, and these deliciously light morsels are a great accompaniment to all the mouthwatering foods you will be preparing for your tea party. My favourite ingredients are tomatoes and goats' cheese; courgette and pine nuts; bacon and cheese; feta, olive and rosemary... in fact, the list is endless. Here's a variation that scores a hit every time.

SPINACH AND PARMESAN
MINI MUFFINS

PREP
15 minutes

COOKING
15–25 minutes

MAKES
16–24 small or
8 large muffins

250g (9oz) plain flour

½ tsp salt

1 tbsp baking powder

1 tsp caster sugar

70g (2½oz) Parmesan cheese (Parmigiano Reggiano
is best), finely grated

100g (3½oz) spinach, cooked, cooled and chopped

1 free-range egg

250ml (9fl oz) milk

90ml (3fl oz) vegetable oil

1 Preheat the oven to 190°C/fan 170°C/gas mark 5. Put mini paper muffin cases into 2 mini muffin tins, or use standard-sized muffin cases and a standard-sized tin.

2 Sift the flour, salt and baking powder into a large mixing bowl. Stir in the sugar, about two-thirds of the Parmesan and the spinach. Set aside.

3 In a large jug, beat together the egg, milk and vegetable oil and pour into the dry ingredients. Using a metal spoon, stir until just combined. Don't beat or stir the mixture too much; it should be quite lumpy, but there should be no traces of dry flour. Spoon the mixture into the muffin cases until about half full, and sprinkle the remaining Parmesan on top.

4 Bake for 15–20 minutes for mini muffins, or 20–25 minutes for standard ones, until you can put a fork into the muffin and it comes out clean.

Making BUTTERFLIES

I first dyed my hair when I was 17. A new hair colour often stems from a need for change and I often compare my journey to that of a butterfly. In the lead-up to finally settling with orange as my 'natural' colour, I've been black, platinum white, fuchsia pink, blue, purple, varying shades of red, mixtures of all the above, and green (although that was an accident).

Who doesn't appreciate the colour and flutter of butterflies? Their delicate, innocent beauty is quite enchanting. A butterfly's journey is impressive: from egg to caterpillar to cocoon to unfurling glory, the butterfly symbolizes change. Change is exciting – it spurs growth and should be embraced. That's why I think this is a great interactive project for friends to work on together at a party. You can cheat and buy ready-made butterflies from all good haberdasheries, but it's not as fun as creating your own.

YOU WILL NEED
for cardboard butterflies

access to a photocopier ✄ paper ✄ glue ✄ thick paper or cardboard ✄ pencil and eraser ✄ black pen ✄ colouring media, such as paints or coloured pencils ✄ scissors

for fabric butterflies

iron ✄ ironing board ✄ thick iron-on interfacing ✄ fabric of your choice ✄ access to a photocopier ✄ paper ✄ scissors ✄ pencil ✄ cardboard ✄ glue

To make cardboard butterflies, use the templates opposite as your starting point. Photocopy the plain or lined butterflies, stick them on to thick paper or cardboard, illustrate if you wish, then paint or colour. Once the paint has dried, cut out your creation, bend in the middle and – voilà – you have a butterfly! Alternatively, why not photocopy our Vintage Patisserie butterflies (opposite, on the far right) and use them as your own?

For fabric butterflies, iron some thick interfacing on to the back of the the fabric. Alternatively, stick the fabric on to cardboard using glue, but be careful of air bubbles when sticking. Photocopy and cut out a selection of the templates opposite, then draw around them on to the interfacing or cardboard. Cut out your creation and bend it in the middle.

When you have a handful of your finest butterflies, look at the following pages for some inspiration for where to stick them!

Rita the Red Admiral

Ringlet Rogers

Adonis Billy Blue

Large Blue Barry

Grizzled Gary

Copper Candy Carol

Grayling Greta

Polly the Purple Emperor

Black Hairstreak Betty

silver-studded Stevie

Mazarine Mae West

swallowtail Sophia

NAME AND FRAME

YOU WILL NEED

an old picture frame ✄ card or material (to mount the butterflies on) ✄ a selection of butterflies ✄ double-sided tape or glue ✄ small plaques for the names

Frames can be incredibly cheap if the picture they carry is somewhat unattractive. Look beyond this and get yourself a bargain. Remove the picture from the frame and cover the inside board with some card or material of your choice. Mount your fabulous butterfly 'friends' using either double-sided tape or glue. Finally, add a plaque under each butterfly. I encourage my friends to design one another's butterflies and then name their work of art. Oh the names I've been called: Orange Marmalade, Copper Candy Carol, Red Betty... I think I'll stop there! This really is a wonderful way to spend some time at any tea party.

WALL OF BUTTERFLIES

YOU WILL NEED

a selection of handmade butterflies in various sizes ✄ a wall space ✄ double-sided tape or glue

Just arrange your butterflies across the wall, starting at the bottom and working up. This project is great fun and so much beauty can be achieved with the help of many hands. I often find myself having to confiscate the butterflies as we have to draw a party to a close!

We all know that fruit smoothies are good for us, but if you are not careful they can taste a little too wholesome! Fat-free yogurt and milk reduces the calories and makes the drink a little lighter. To make this drink more substantial and sweet, try adding some banana or honey.

The old wives' tale tells us that eating carrots helps your eyesight, but sometimes larger carrots are not so tasty and there are only so many one can eat in a sitting. The apples really lift this drink and the ginger adds a nice little bit of heat. Obviously, such a lovely drink cannot be stirred with anything other than a crisp little baby carrot!

TRIPLE BERRY SMOOTHIE

PREP
5 minutes

SERVES
6–8

600ml (1 pint) fat-free vanilla yogurt

100ml (3½fl oz) fat-free milk or soy milk

150g (5½oz) blueberries

70g (2½oz) blackberries

70g (2½oz) raspberries

fresh mint and a few extra berries, to decorate

1 Put the yogurt, milk and berries in a blender and blend on high speed until smooth (about 1 minute).

2 Pour and serve immediately, decorated with extra berries and mint leaves.

ALL THE BETTER FOR SEEING YOU

PREP
5–10 minutes

SERVES 4

10 carrots, roughly chopped

5 apples, cored and roughly chopped

2.5cm (1in) square piece of ginger, peeled

ice cubes

4 baby carrots, to serve

1 Juice the carrots, apples and ginger together and serve in teacups over ice – with a baby carrot to stir, of course.

In my fantasy world, everything would be ruby-coloured. When I make this drink, I taste it first with my eyes. I adore the magnificent deep colour and the earthy taste. Be warned, though: the flavour of the beetroot is so intense that it needs to be tempered with the other fruit and vegetables.

RUbY DeL-icious

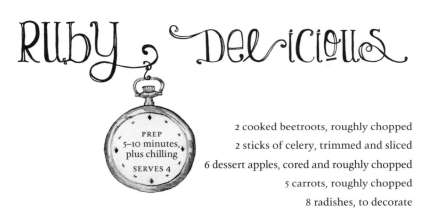

PREP
5–10 minutes,
plus chilling

SERVES 4

2 cooked beetroots, roughly chopped

2 sticks of celery, trimmed and sliced

6 dessert apples, cored and roughly chopped

5 carrots, roughly chopped

8 radishes, to decorate

1 Juice all the ingredients except the radishes.

2 To make radish roses, cut 4 thin vertical slices around the outside of the radish with a small knife, making sure not to cut all the way through. Repeat this process but each time offset the slice from the previous one moving closer to the top of the radish. Once this is done, place the radishes in a bowl of iced water and leave in the refrigerator for 2–3 hours.

3 Serve the juice in teacups, each decorated with a couple of radish roses.

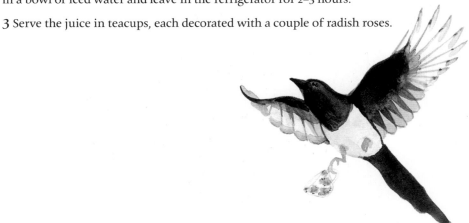

All The Better For Seeing You

Triple Berry smoothie

Ruby Delicious

Pomegranates really epitomize the saying 'It's what's on the inside that counts'. They look so boring on the outside, but when you open them up you are welcomed by those beautiful ruby-coloured jewels. The crunch of the seeds, along with the slight bitterness, is unique and works very well with sweet tea. Squeezing the juice takes a little effort, but the extra freshness makes it worthwhile.

POMEGRANATE iced Tea

PREP
5–10 minutes,
plus chilling

SERVES 4

300ml (½ pint) black tea, sweetened to taste

125ml (4fl oz) freshly squeezed pomegranate juice
(use store-bought juice if time is an issue)

ice cubes

seeds from ½ fresh pomegranate, to decorate

1 Make the tea as you would normally and refrigerate until cool.

2 Mix the chilled tea into the pomegranate juice, add some ice cubes and serve decorated with a sprinkling of pomegranate seeds.

Health experts often say that lemon is the best thing to have in the morning. So, with our health in mind, I have created a lovely morning kick-starter. The blend of the acidic oranges and lemons, the hint of mint and the sweet tea are delicious. This is also a great palate cleanser, and so much nicer than plain lemon iced tea. If you want to be creative, you can freeze the mint inside the ice cubes.

CITRUS iced tea

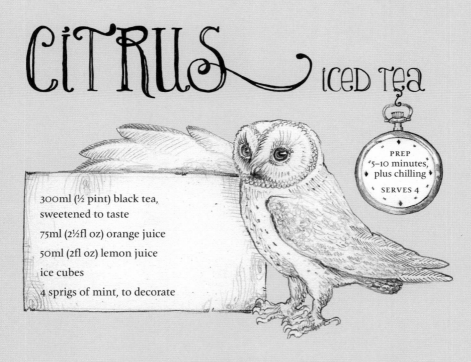

PREP
5–10 minutes,
plus chilling

SERVES 4

300ml (½ pint) black tea, sweetened to taste

75ml (2½fl oz) orange juice

50ml (2fl oz) lemon juice

ice cubes

4 sprigs of mint, to decorate

1 Make the tea as you would normally and refrigerate until cool.

2 Mix the chilled tea with the orange and lemon juice, add some ice cubes and serve decorated with mint sprigs.

This Scottish classic is so luxurious and rich that you will feel positively guilty drinking it. The quantities of whisky and honey can be adjusted and I recommend adding a little grated nutmeg to the cream. The first time I tasted this, I wondered why the Scots ever decided to eat porridge for breakfast.

I can't lie about my relationship with cider. It reminds me of my younger days. But as an adult I've fallen in love with it again and I adore the sharp but feminine taste the raspberries add to this drink. It is a naughty start to a lazy day off and the perfect brunch drink to enjoy with friends. Use apple juice for a non-alcoholic version.

ATHOL BROSE
MORNING DRINK

PREP
10–15 minutes
SERVES 4

generous handful of pinhead oatmeal

400ml (14fl oz) single cream

1 tbsp honey

3 tbsp whisky

HOT RASPBERRY AND APPLE DRINK

PREP
5–10 minutes
COOKING
12–15 minutes
SERVES 8

1 litre (1¾ pints) cider or apple juice

125ml (4fl oz) raspberry juice

30g (1oz) caster sugar, or to taste

9 cinnamon sticks

1 Toast the oatmeal in a dry frying pan over a medium heat until golden brown, then allow to cool in a sieve.

2 Heat the cream in a saucepan over a medium heat until warm (be careful not to let it boil), then remove from the heat.

3 Mix the honey and whisky together, then add them to the cream.

4 Pour into espresso cups and serve at once with the toasted oatmeal sprinkled on the top.

1 Combine the cider or apple juice, raspberry juice and sugar in a saucepan, add 1 cinnamon stick and stir over a medium heat until the sugar dissolves and the mixture starts to simmer. Allow to simmer for 10 minutes.

2 Remove from the heat, then take out the cinnamon stick. Serve warm, adding a fresh cinnamon stick to each glass for stirring.

WARNING: this is nothing like the bland Mocha you get in your local chain coffee shop. When it is made slowly like this, the flavours meld together and the taste is positively decadent.

WHITE CHOCOLATE Mocha

PREP
5–10 minutes
SERVES 4–6

500ml (18fl oz) whole or semi-skimmed milk

55g (2oz) white chocolate

500ml (18fl oz) freshly brewed coffee

whipped cream and white chocolate sprinkles, to decorate

1 Pour the milk into a small saucepan and grate the white chocolate into it. Stir over a medium–low heat until the chocolate melts, then remove from the heat.

2 Add the coffee and stir. Pour into vintage teacups, top with whipped cream and a sprinkling of white chocolate and serve immediately.

White Chocolate Mocha

Hot Raspberry and Apple Dr

Athol Brose Morning Drink

AFTERNOON

Afternoon Contents

Features

Let's raise our teacups and pay homage to Anna Maria, the seventh Duchess of Bedford, for introducing us to the 'Afternoon Tea'.

In the mid-19th century, Anna Maria simply could not bear the hiatus between lunch and dinner and insisted she was brought tea and cakes between 2 and 5pm to stop her hunger pains. Oh, how we are kindred spirits!

We Brits are incredibly proud of our tea tradition, and since 1868, when Queen Victoria held her first Royal Tea Party at Buckingham Palace, we have been unstoppable.

This chapter is a nod to tradition, bringing some colour into the past and ensuring you are sporting the right hair decoration to erect your pinkie finger and say 'Cheers!'

Afternoon tea is not complete without a plate of dainty, freshly made crustless sandwiches. I like to use a variety of fillings, ranging from the traditional (such as egg mayonnaise, or ham and mustard) to something a bit more modern (such as radish, smoked salmon or roast beef). You must always use the freshest bread – as the sandwiches have to be pillow soft – and real salted butter. I like to stick with tradition and serve my sandwiches in triangles, but feel free to experiment; you can cut them into squares or fingers, or even serve them as open sandwiches trussed up as bunting!

BUNTING BUTTIES

THE PERFECT EGG SANDWICH

FOR EACH VARIETY
PREP & COOKING
25 minutes
MAKES 24

6 free-range eggs
6 tbsp mayonnaise
salt and black pepper
25g (1oz) butter, at room temperature
12 slices of soft bread (white or brown)
1 tub of mustard and cress

1 Place the eggs in a saucepan of cold water. Bring the water to boiling point, remove from the heat immediately, cover with a lid and leave to stand for 13 minutes. Transfer the eggs to cold water to stop the cooking process.

2 Once cooled, peel the eggs, then chop them finely. Mix with the mayonnaise and season to taste.

3 Butter the bread, then spread the egg mayonnaise over 6 of the slices. Sprinkle with the mustard and cress and top with the remaining bread slices. Cut off the crusts with a serrated bread knife, cut each round diagonally into 4 sandwiches and serve immediately.

RADISH TEA SANDWICHES

150g (5½oz) radishes, topped and tailed
1 tsp poppy seeds
150g (5½oz) cream cheese
salt
25g (1oz) butter, at room temperature
12 slices of soft bread (white, brown or a mixture)

1 Either chop the radishes very finely or mince them in a food processor. Combine them in a bowl with the poppy seeds, cream cheese and salt, and blend well.

2 Butter the bread, then spread the radish filling over 6 of the slices. Top with the remaining slices. Cut off the crusts with a serrated bread knife, cut each round diagonally into 4 sandwiches and serve immediately.

RARE BEEF AND HOMEMADE HORSERADISH SANDWICHES

25g (1oz) butter, at room temperature
12 slices of soft bread (white or brown)
6 tsp Horseradish Cream (see below)
6 slices of rare roast beef

For the horseradish cream
100g (3½oz) finely grated horseradish
150ml (5fl oz) crème fraîche
1 tbsp red wine vinegar
salt and pepper

1 To make the horseradish cream, combine all the ingredients thoroughly in a mixing bowl. This sauce keeps for several days in the refrigerator.

2 Butter the bread, then spread a thin layer of horseradish cream on 6 of the slices. Top with the roast beef, spread with more cream, then cover with the remaining bread slices. Cut off the crusts with a serrated bread knife, cut each round diagonally into 4 sandwiches and serve immediately.

Afternoon tea traditionalists will tell you that cucumber sandwiches are a must on a sandwich platter. Well, to be honest, I find them a tad boring, so I've come up with an Angel Adoree version that is pretty to behold and lovely to eat. You can ring the changes by using a different type of cream cheese and varying the sandwich shape.

CReAM CHeeSe AND CUCUMBeR HeARTS

PREP
10 minutes

MAKES 24

2 small cucumbers

6 slices of soft white bread

15g (½oz) butter, at room temperature

150g (5½oz) cream cheese

salt

1 Top and tail the cucumbers. Using a vegetable peeler, peel 4 strips from the length of each cucumber (one strip on each 'side'). Discard these. Next, peel 12 more strips from the peeled faces of each cucumber (each strip should still have a narrow edge of skin). Cut each strip in half widthways. Set aside.

2 Spread each slice of bread with butter and then with cream cheese, and season with a sprinkling of salt.

3 Lay 4 overlapping strips of cucumber across each slice of bread to cover the cheese. Using a small heart-shaped cutter, cut 4 hearts from each slice of bread. Discard the remains. Serve immediately.

HOW TO DRY
EDIBLE FLOWERS

One of my first baking memories is of making rosewater biscuits with my grandmother. I loved the aroma of the rosewater so much that I tried to drink it (I must say, don't try that at home!). My obsession with roses continues now that I'm a grown-up woman, and wherever possible I cook with the pretty little petals, which can be added to salads and cakes, or used as decorations. The bright colours and subtle flavours are marvellous.

If you want to grow edible flowers yourself, be sure never to treat them with pesticides or other chemicals, which are poisonous. Sadly, if you buy flowers from a florist, you should assume that they have been sprayed with these nasties. If you are unable to grow flowers yourself you will, with a little help from the trusty internet, chance upon companies that specialize in dried edible flowers.

Here's a step-by-step guide to drying petals from homegrown flowers.

STEP 1 Select your flowers and remove their petals carefully (use only the petals).

STEP 2 Give the petals a good wash using cold water. I wash them like salad by placing them in a strainer in a bowl of water.

STEP 3 Drain the water and place the petals on kitchen paper to soak up any excess water. Make sure the petals are not left out in direct sunlight because the colours will fade – the petals should preserve their colours and scent if they dry quickly.

STEP 4 You might also like to slip the petals into a small lingerie or mesh bag so they are able to dry. Hang the petals in a dark, dry room, such as a larder cupboard.

STEP 5 Dry the petals for around 24 hours. It's a good idea to dry them overnight so that they are ready the next day.

You can eat the following flowers:

lavender 🌹 carnation 🌹 safflower 🌹 marigold 🌹 cornflower

rose 🌹 mimosa 🌹 violet 🌹 gerbera

Marigold

Cornflower

Mauve Rose

Mint

Red Carnation

Sugared Mimosa

Hot Pink Rose

Flower Petal Blend

Aubergine Rose

If you are looking for indulgence or just an interesting talking point, the rose petal sandwich could be just the thing. These delicacies may not be everyone's cup of tea, but isn't it good to try something you can't pick up in your local supermarket once in a while? Rose petal sandwiches were popular during the years leading up to World War II. Mine is a slightly more modern take on the classic but, trust me, it's rosy delicious – these sandwiches taste divine, will raise a few eyebrows and look gorgeous, too.

ROSE PETAL sandwiches

PREP
10 minutes,
plus soaking

MAKES 24

60 dried organic rose petals (available on the internet)

few drops of rose essence

25g (1oz) butter, at room temperature

12 slices of soft white bread

6 tsp lavender honey

1 Soak the dried rose petals in a bowl of cold water with the rose essence for 20 minutes (this rehydrates the petal and gives it more flavour) then drain and set aside.

2 Butter the bread, then spread the honey over 6 of the slices.

3 Divide the rose petals between the 6 slices of honeyed bread and top with the remaining bread slices. Cut off the crusts with a serrated bread knife, cut each round diagonally into 4 sandwiches and serve immediately.

Jam sandwiches take me back to the time when I was a little girl. As an afternoon-tea snack, my grandmother would slice up some fresh white bread and spread it thickly with some golden butter and sweet strawberry jam. I would sit happy and contented, munching the sandwich with a glass of cold milk. This is an updated version of a happy childhood memory. Use different types of jam for maximum visual effect.

Lollipop Jam Sandwiches

PREP
15 minutes,
plus cooling

MAKES 30

6 slices of soft bread (white, brown or a mixture)

15g (½oz) butter, at room temperature

3 tbsp jam (apricot, strawberry, blackcurrant or a mixture)

1 Flatten each of the bread slices with a rolling pin, then slice the crusts off with a serrated bread knife.

2 Carefully spread each slice with butter and then jam, making sure that the fillings do not overlap the edges of the bread.

3 Using both hands, roll up each slice into a sausage. Wrap each sausage tightly in clingfilm and tie each end in a knot. Place the sausages in the refrigerator for 30 minutes to firm them.

4 Remove the sausages from the refrigerator, untie the ends and peel off the clingfilm. Slice 5 pinwheels from each sausage (discard the ends, which tend to be a bit messy). Insert a cocktail stick into each sandwich to secure it. Serve immediately.

Savoury Creams and Butters

Before I go out to dine, I repeat a mantra to myself: 'Lady, stay away from the bread.' This is not because I'm watching my waistline, but just because sometimes you can get carried away. I'm sure most people can relate to this. Well-made warm bread spread with melting butter is much like a hug and, if eaten in moderation, it's a real treat. I flavour my butters and creams with all sorts of ingredients; below are some great ideas to inspire you to experiment further.

Flavoured Butter

This is a simple trick that looks great at a dinner table (it's all in the detail). Enjoy it with bread, vegetables or meats. Simply delicious!

PREP
5 minutes,
plus chilling
SERVES 8

250g (9oz) butter, at room temperature

Your choice of the following:

handful of thyme and 1 tsp salt

handful of chopped chives

handful of chopped parsley and grated rind of 2 lemons

handful of chopped sage and 1 tsp wholegrain mustard

handful of chopped tarragon and ½ tsp vanilla extract

4 garlic cloves, crushed

3 small bird's eye chillies, chopped

1 Mix the butter with your chosen filling. Spoon into a piece of clingfilm and roll into a sausage shape.

2 Place in the refrigerator to harden.

3 When ready to use, remove the clingfilm and cut into slices to serve.

Flavoured Crème Fraîche

Flavoured crème fraîche is a great alternative to flavoured butter. It's cleaner, but still rich and creamy. This is my favourite combination, but why not also try smoked salmon and lemon rind, artichoke and red pepper, or basil and tomato with black pepper?

Beetroot and Horseradish Cream

PREP
10–15 minutes
COOKING
30–40 minutes
SERVES 8

2 large raw beetroots, washed, trimmed and quartered or cut into 5cm (2in) cubes

2 tbsp extra-virgin olive oil

4 tbsp crème fraîche

1–2 tsp Horseradish Cream (*see* page 109)

30g (1oz) pack of chives, finely chopped

1 Preheat the oven to 180°C/fan 160°C/gas mark 4. Place the beetroot in a roasting tin, drizzle with olive oil and roast in the oven for 30–40 minutes until tender.

2 Blitz the beetroot in a food processor until smooth then mix in the crème fraîche, horseradish and chives.

The word 'roulade' comes from the French word *rouler*, meaning 'to roll'. Roulades look incredibly professional, so whenever I can roll, I do! Often it's the way you roll that gives this dish the wow factor. Smoked trout is used here as a lighter alternative to salmon, and it goes really well with the creamy filling. If you don't like horseradish you can leave it out, but it's definitely worth a try.

SMOKED TROUT and CREAM CHEESE ROULADE

PREP
15–25 minutes,
plus 1 hour
chilling

SERVES 6

250g (9oz) cream cheese
handful of chives, chopped
30g (1oz) Horseradish Cream
(*see* page 109)
200g (7oz) smoked trout, sliced

1 In a bowl, mix together the cream cheese, chives and Horseradish Cream. You want a delicate flavour, so start cautiously, taste and add more Horseradish Cream if you think you'd like something a bit stronger. Set aside.

2 Place overlapping slices of smoked trout in the middle of a sheet of clingfilm to make a rectangle of about 15 × 20cm (6 × 8in). Very gently spread the cheese mixture on to the smoked trout – you want a layer about 3–4mm (⅛in) thick.

3 To roll the trout, take hold of the clingfilm along the long edge of your rectangle and lift it up and slightly over until the edge of the trout starts to roll over. Carefully continue to roll the fish 'Swiss roll'. When you have got the finished roulade, wrap it in clingfilm and chill for 1 hour. Remove the clingfilm and slice just before serving.

Tall FILO BASKETS with STILTON, PEAR and WALNUTS

PREP
30 minutes

COOKING
7 minutes

MAKES 12

I like to combine contrasting flavours and textures in my recipes, and this one is no exception. The silky-sweet pears perfectly balance the saltiness of the Stilton, and the walnuts and filo pastry provide a nice crunch. I prefer to use ripe pears as they are often sweeter and juicier than the firmer ones. Alternative fillings that you might like to try are: roasted tomato with goats' cheese; Cheddar cheese with pickled onions; pancetta, pea and mint; and roasted shallot, red pepper and smoked sausage.

1 Preheat the oven to 220°C/fan 200°C/gas mark 7.

2 Unroll the filo pastry and, using a sharp knife, cut each sheet into 8, so you have 48 10cm (4in) squares. Using a pastry brush, brush one side of each square with melted butter. To make the pastry baskets, lay 1 square on top of another at a 45-degree angle so the points are offset. Then add a 3rd and 4th square, arranging the points to fall where those of the first two squares fell, so you end up with a 4-layered star shape. When you have finished you should have 12 baskets.

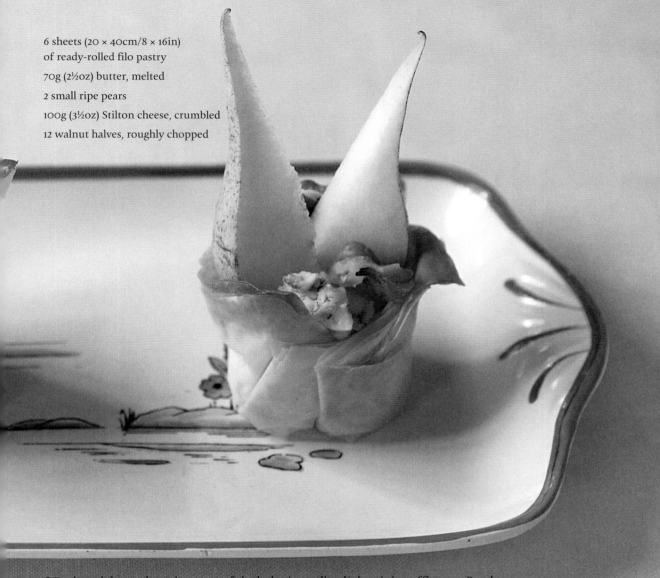

6 sheets (20 × 40cm/8 × 16in)
of ready-rolled filo pastry

70g (2½oz) butter, melted

2 small ripe pears

100g (3½oz) Stilton cheese, crumbled

12 walnut halves, roughly chopped

3 Push each layered star into one of the holes in a tall 12-hole mini-muffin pan. Brush the edges with any remaining melted butter.

4 Bake the pastry baskets for 7 minutes, until golden. Allow to cool in the muffin pan.

5 Quarter the pears and remove their cores. Slice each quarter into 3 lengthways, then arrange 2 slices of pear in each pastry basket. Divide the crumbled Stilton evenly between the baskets, then do the same with the chopped walnuts.

6 Serve the baskets either individually or on a large serving plate.

I adore the simplicity of this recipe. The presentation takes a little bit of time, but your guests will love this different take on the ubiquitous tomato and mozzarella starter. I put the oil and vinegar in shot glasses – but I have to make sure that no one drinks any of them!

TOMATO MOZZARELLA balls

PREP
15 minutes
MAKES 24

24 sprigs of basil
24 mini plum tomatoes
24 mini mozzarella pearls
black pepper (optional)
extra-virgin olive oil and balsamic vinegar, for dipping

1 Carefully thread the basil sprigs on to 24 cocktail or kebab sticks.

2 Cut the pointed base off each tomato and thread one tomato on to each stick behind the basil, cut-side up.

3 Thread a mozzarella pearl on to each stick, to sit on top of the tomato.

4 Sprinkle with black pepper, if you like, and serve with olive oil and balsamic vinegar.

These mini baked potatoes are always the surprising star dish at my tea parties. People seem to relish the simplicity of a comforting warm potato slathered with sour cream. They are a favourite of mine, too, and I sometimes I have to stop myself tasting too many of them when I set up for a party.

THE BRITISH POTATO

PREP
5 minutes

COOKING
20 minutes

MAKES 12

12 new potatoes

extra-virgin olive oil

sea salt and black pepper

4 tbsp soured cream

small pack of chives, chopped, to garnish

1 Preheat the oven to 220°C/fan 200°C/gas mark 7.

2 Toss the potatoes in a little olive oil and season to taste. Place in a roasting tin and bake for 20 minutes, or until they are tender and the skins have turned golden brown.

3 Cut a cross into the top of each potato and top with a teaspoonful of the soured cream. Garnish with chopped chives, then serve immediately.

THE
BRITISH
POTATO
QUEEN ELIZABETH II
1952
1977
SILVER
JUBILEE

No afternoon tea is complete without the quintessentially British scone. When served warm with thick clotted cream and luscious strawberry jam, there's nothing quite like it. A fabulous elderly lady once told me that my scones were better than those at the Ritz! They are quick and easy to make, so do give it a go. Here's my basic recipe, but feel free to add other ingredients. Raisins, cinnamon and even chocolate chips would be lovely additions.

CLASSIC SCONE recipe

PREP
20 minutes

COOKING
16–18 minutes

MAKES 10

70g (2½oz) butter, at room temperature, plus extra for greasing

250g (9oz) plain flour

50g (1¾oz) caster sugar

2 tsp baking powder

¼ tsp salt

125ml (4fl oz) milk

1 large free-range egg, lightly beaten

1 tsp vanilla extract

a little egg and/or milk, for glazing

Quick Strawberry Jam (*see* page 84) and clotted cream, to serve

1 Preheat the oven to 220°C/fan 200°C/gas mark 7. Lightly grease a baking sheet with butter.

2 In a large bowl, mix all the dry ingredients together. Using your fingers, crumble the butter into the mixture until it is evenly distributed, then (still using your hands) gently fold in the milk, egg and vanilla extract. The key is not to mix too much, as mixing will take the air out. Once everything has bound together, separate the mixture into small balls, place these on the prepared baking sheet and glaze with egg, milk or a mixture of both.

3 Bake in the oven for 16–18 minutes, until golden brown. Serve warm with my Quick Strawberry Jam and clotted cream.

This is a delicious citrus twist on the Classic Scone Recipe. I like to keep my scones looking rustic, so I hand-roll the dough into small balls. As an alternative to (or as well as) the lavender cream, these scones are super served hot with clotted cream and my Quick Strawberry Jam (*see* page 84).

LEMON SCONES WITH LAVENDER CREAM

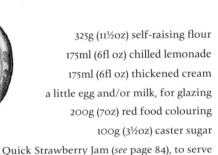

PREP
20 minutes

COOKING
12–15 minutes

MAKES
20–24

325g (11½oz) self-raising flour

175ml (6fl oz) chilled lemonade

175ml (6fl oz) thickened cream

a little egg and/or milk, for glazing

200g (7oz) red food colouring

100g (3½oz) caster sugar

Quick Strawberry Jam (*see* page 84), to serve

For the lavender cream

200ml (7fl oz) double cream

200ml (7fl oz) crème fraîche

1 tbsp lavender honey

handful of culinary lavender, for sprinkling

1 Preheat the oven to 200°C/fan 180°C/gas mark 6. Line 2 baking sheets with nonstick baking paper. Sift the flour into a large bowl. In a separate bowl combine the lemonade and cream, then fold this together with the flour.

2 Divide the dough into 20–24 small balls and place on the prepared baking sheets, leaving about 2.5cm (1in) between them. Glaze with egg, milk or a mixture of both. Add a few drops of red food colouring to the sugar and sprinkle over the scones. Bake for about 12–15 minutes or until pale golden and cooked through. If you like your scones to have a soft crust, cover them with a clean tea towel for 1 minute after removing them from the oven.

3 For the lavender cream, fold the cream, crème fraîche and honey together and sprinkle with the culinary lavender. Serve with the warm scones and Quick Strawberry Jam.

I do love my sweet treats but there are times when something savoury is called for, and these delicious scones fit the bill. Feel free to ring in the changes with different cheeses and nuts. You could also add some chopped herbs, sunblush tomatoes, tiny bits of fried onion, or cooked bacon lardons. Like their sweet counterparts, these savoury scones are a doddle to make.

Brie and Walnut Savoury Scones

PREP
20 minutes

COOKING
16–18 minutes

MAKES 10

70g (2½oz) butter, at room temperature, plus extra for greasing

250g (9oz) plain flour

2 tsp baking powder

¼ tsp salt

125ml (4fl oz) milk

1 large free-range egg, lightly beaten

125g (4½oz) Brie, cut into small pieces

100g (3½oz) walnuts, broken into pieces

a little egg and/or milk, for glazing

1 Preheat the oven to 220°C/fan 200°C/gas mark 7. Lightly grease a baking sheet with butter.

2 In a large bowl, mix all the dry ingredients together. Using your fingers, crumble the butter into the mixture until it is evenly distributed, then (still using your hands) gently fold in the milk and egg. The key to this recipe is not to mix too much, as mixing will take the air out. Once everything has bound together, separate the mixture into 10 small balls and place these on the prepared baking sheet.

3 Divide the Brie and walnut pieces between the scones and press them gently into the top of the dough to embed them. Glaze with egg, milk or a mixture of both.

4 Bake for 16–18 minutes, until golden brown. Serve warm.

Hair Decorations

'Where did you get that hat? Where did you get that tile? Isn't it a nobby one, and just the proper style? I should like to have one just the same as that!'

The answer to the first question above is, 'I made it'.

Headgear is an extension of one's style, mood and personality. Since the late 17th century, women have been decorating their heads. Marie Antoinette was renowned for wearing just about anything on her head, Lilly Daché bought us elegance, and Isabella Blow took us to the future. Glue guns at the ready, everyone?

MAKING A HAT

YOU WILL NEED

pinking shears ✄ small pieces of fabric about 10 × 10cm
(4 × 4in) ✄ sinamay or straw fascinator bases ✄ glue gun
✄ small crocodile or curl clips ✄ a variety of decorative
items (including feathers, beads, jewels, pompoms, butterflies
(*see* pages 90–91) and small decorative feathered birds (a trip to
your local haberdashery will unearth a world of treasures)

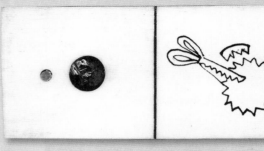

STEP 1 Cut a small circle of fabric, bigger than your chosen clip, but smaller than your fascinator base.

STEP 2 Apply a small amount hot glue to the top of the clip

STEP 3 Stick the top of the glued clip to the underside of the fascinator. You may want to have a play around to see where the best position for the clip would be. For example, on a teardrop-shaped base the curved end would be the best positioning so that the finished hair decoration can be clipped into the hair from back to front.

STEP 4 Apply hot glue 1cm (½in) from the edge of the fabric circle.

STEP 5 Using one hand to hold the clip open, insert the fabric between the prongs, glue-side down, and press gently to the underside of the hat.

STEP 6 Finally, use your imagination and decorate your hat in any weird or wonderful way you wish.

I often use the internet as a source of recipe ideas and food styling, but only once have I found a recipe that is both unique and so unbelievably tasty that I just want to leave it in its original state. This cake is always a big hit at my parties; I love the twist that the heavenly sweet and fragrant pomegranate arils lend to the classic carrot cake.

CARAMELIZED POMEGRANATE AND CARROT CAKE

PREP
30 minutes

COOKING
50–55 minutes

MAKES
18cm (7in) square
cake

1 Preheat the oven to 180°C/fan 160°C/gas mark 4 and grease a 18cm (7in) square baking tin.

2 To caramelize the pomegranate seeds, melt the butter in a pan over a low heat and add the fresh ginger and spices. When their aromas have released, stir in the pomegranate seeds and sugar. Add the water and slowly reduce to a sticky syrup texture, stirring. Set aside.

3 To make the cake, combine the flour, bicarbonate of soda, baking powder, salt and sugar in a large bowl. In another bowl, whisk the oil, eggs and yogurt, then combine with the flour mixture, carrot and caramelized pomegranate seeds, being careful not to over-mix.

4 Pour the batter into the prepared tin and bake for about 40–45 minutes, until it turns golden brown. Test with a toothpick – the cake is done when the pick comes out (almost) clean.

5 Serve in triangles decorated with dollops of cream cheese, baby carrots and a sprinkling of cayenne pepper.

125ml (4fl oz) vegetable oil, plus extra for greasing

150g (5½oz) plain flour

½ tsp bicarbonate of soda

¾ tsp baking powder

pinch of salt

225g (8oz) caster sugar

2 large free-range eggs

3 tbsp natural yogurt

350ml (12fl oz) finely shredded (juicy) carrot

For the caramelized pomegranate seeds

1 tbsp butter

1 tsp diced fresh ginger

½ tsp ground cinnamon

seeds of 1 crushed green cardamom pod

115g (4oz) pomegranate seeds (you can buy these ready prepared in the supermarket, or remove the seeds from roughly 3–4 pomegranates)

2 tbsp caster sugar

15ml (½fl oz) water

To decorate

100g (3½oz) cream cheese

6–8 baby carrots

cayenne pepper

This is an unexpected crowd-pleaser at my tea parties. It is an unassuming butter cake, but the addition of apples and a crumble topping turns it into something special. Serve it warm with vanilla ice cream or cold with a mug of tea. The key to success is to whisk the eggs and sugar long enough for them to hold the crumble in suspension. Don't be tempted to rush this stage. Check there is a trail on the surface of the egg mixture when you lift the whisk before adding the other ingredients.

Apple Crumble cake

PREP
30 minutes
COOKING
50–55 minutes
SERVES 12

250g (9oz) butter, plus extra for greasing

250g (9oz) caster sugar

250g (9oz) self-raising flour, sifted

4 free-range eggs

3 small dessert apples, peeled, cored and thinly sliced

1 Preheat the oven to 180°C/fan 160°C/gas mark 4. Grease and line the base of a 23cm (9in) round, deep cake tin.

2 To make the crumble topping, measure 50g (1¾oz) each of the sugar and butter and 60g (2¼oz) of the flour into a bowl. Rub together with your fingertips until it forms a rough crumble. Set aside.

3 Put the remaining sugar in a large bowl with the eggs and whisk together with an electric whisk for 10 minutes, until the mixture is pale and thick. Melt the remaining butter in a pan, allow to cool slightly then, using the whisk on its lowest setting to combine, drizzle the butter slowly into the whisked mixture. Fold in the remaining flour.

4 Turn the mixture into the prepared tin and arrange the apple slices evenly over the top. Sprinkle with the crumble and bake for 50–55 minutes, until the cake is firm to the touch and golden brown. Allow to cool for 10 minutes in the tin before turning it out and serving warm.

Sometimes the best things in life are the simplest, like this gorgeous, sun-kissed lemon tart. A wonderful fresh lemon scent wafts through the kitchen when I bake it, and I often find myself tapping my foot, impatiently waiting for it to cook. A good dollop of crème fraîche or thick clotted cream is the perfect accompaniment to the rich sweet tang of the tart.

LEMON TART

* PREP *
25 minutes
COOKING
25–30 minutes
SERVES 6–8

For the filling

3 free-range eggs

4 tbsp lemon juice

225–280g (8–10oz) caster sugar

1 tbsp grated orange rind

55g (2oz) butter, melted

generous 100g (3½oz) plain flour

40g (1½oz) icing sugar, plus extra to decorate

70g (2½oz) ground almonds

1 tsp grated lemon rind

1 tsp grated orange rind

generous 100g (3½oz) cold butter

100ml (3½fl oz) crème fraîche and a handful of fresh raspberries, to decorate

1 Preheat the oven to 180°C/fan 160°C/gas mark 4. To make the filling, place the eggs, lemon juice, sugar and orange rind in a blender. Cover and blend at high speed until smooth. Add the butter, cover and process on high until just smooth. Set aside.

2 To make the pastry, place the flour, icing sugar, almonds, lemon rind, orange rind and butter in a food processor. Cover and process until the mixture forms a ball. Press the pastry on to the bottom and up the sides of an ungreased 23cm (9in) round fluted tart tin with a removable base.

3 Pour the filling into the pastry. Bake for 25–30 minutes or until the centre is almost set. Cool in the tin on a wire rack then remove to a serving plate.

4 Just before serving, sprinkle with icing sugar and decorate each slice with a teaspoonful of crème fraîche and a fresh raspberry.

Bittersweet Chocolate
Pear Cake

Lemon Tart

range Eccles Cakes

'When is a cake not a cake? When it's an Eccles cake!' My grandfather loved saying this each time my gran brought out a plate of these delicious homemade goodies when I visited. He was right, too; an Eccles cake is actually a pastry. I have brought my gran's recipe up to date with the addition of some orange rind. A dredging of sugar on these cakes gives a good crunch.

orange Eccles cakes

PREP
25 minutes,
plus soaking

COOKING
10 minutes

MAKES 6

115g (4oz) currants

4 tbsp orange liqueur

finely grated rind of 1 orange

175g (6oz) ready-made puff pastry

plain flour, for dusting

25g (1oz) butter

granulated sugar, for sprinkling

1 free-range egg, beaten

candied peel, to decorate

1 Combine the currants, orange liqueur and rind in a bowl, cover and leave for 24 hours, or until the fruit is plump and has absorbed all the liqueur.

2 Preheat the oven to 180°C/fan 160°C/gas mark 4. Using a rolling pin, roll out the puff pastry on a lightly floured surface until it is nice and thin and then cut into 6 rounds the size of a tumbler, about 6cm (2½in) in diameter.

3 Place a scant teaspoonful of marinated currants in the middle of a round, then add a very small piece of butter and a sprinkling of sugar. Brush the outer edge of the pastry with the egg, then gather the pastry rim together in the centre and pinch to seal the filling. Turn the cake over, then roll it gently with a rolling pin, just until the cake is slightly flattened. Continue with the other rounds of pastry until all the ingredients are used up.

4 Place the cakes on a baking sheet and brush with more egg. Sprinkle with sugar, make a cut in the top of each cake and decorate with candied peel. Bake for about 10 minutes, or until the pastry is golden brown. Remove the Eccles cakes from the oven, allow them to cool slightly and serve warm.

One of the happiest culinary marriages is between chocolate and pear, and it's one of my favourite combinations, too, so you can imagine how much I adore this cake. It's amazing, to say the least! The pear keeps the cake moist while the chocolate lends a lovely taste and texture contrast. The surprise ingredient is the burnt butter, which provides a smoky nuttiness.

Bittersweet Chocolate Pear Cake

PREP
15–25 minutes

COOKING
45–55 minutes

SERVES 8

115g (4oz) butter, plus extra for greasing

100g (3½oz) plain flour, plus extra for dusting

1 tbsp baking powder

3 free-range eggs

175g (6oz) caster sugar

4 small pears, diced, plus 1 small pear, sliced, to decorate

175g (6oz) dark chocolate, broken into pieces, plus extra, grated, to decorate

100ml (3½fl oz) crème fraîche, to decorate

1 Preheat the oven to 180°C/fan 160°C/gas mark 4.

2 Butter and flour a 23cm (9in) springform cake tin. In a small bowl, sift together the flour and baking powder. Set aside. In a large bowl, whisk the eggs with an electric whisk until they are pale and very thick. Set aside.

3 Heat the butter over a medium heat in a medium-sized saucepan, until browned. As it cooks, it will foam up. Stir occasionally and scrape the solids off the bottom of the pan as they accumulate. (The butter goes from browned to burnt in less than a minute, so watch it closely.) When browned, remove from the heat and pour into a separate bowl. Set aside.

4 Add the sugar to the eggs and continue whisking for a few more minutes.

5 When the eggs start to lose their volume, change the speed on the whisk to low and add one-third of the flour mixture, then half the melted butter, one-third of the flour, the remainder of the butter and the remainder of the flour. Mix until barely combined to avoid losing more volume.

6 Pour the batter into the prepared tin and arrange the diced pears and dark chocolate on top. Bake for 40–50 minutes or until the cake is a light golden brown colour. Test the cake by inserting a toothpick into the centre of the cake – if it comes out clean, the cake is ready.

7 Let the cake cool in the tin for 10 minutes, then transfer to a cooling rack. Serve each slice warm, decorated with a teaspoonful of crème fraîche, a pear slice and some grated dark chocolate.

BiRD MobiLE

'Good Morning Mr Magpie, where is your lovely wife today?'

Birdwatching is a fascinating pastime. Here at the Vintage Patisserie we flood our tea-party tables with birds: red robins, blackbirds, blue tits, swallows, ravens, tawny owls, yellowhammers… the list goes on and on. If you fancy bringing some of Mother Nature's favourites into your home, this is a fast and fabulous way to do it.

YOU WILL NEED

bird images ✀ paper ✀ craft knife or scissors ✀ spray adhesive or glue stick ✀ foam board ✀ needle ✀ fishing wire ✀ twigs or chandelier, for hanging

STEP 1 Select your bird images and print them out. Mirror each image digitally and print a second copy so your mobile pieces will be double-sided.

STEP 2 Take your set of images and make sure that both sides match up. Trim around each piece, leaving a border around the edge of the images to take into consideration complex outlines of feathers. This will give your pieces a neater finish when they are all hanging together.

STEP 3 Apply adhesive to the image for the first side of each bird and mount on to foam board. Make sure that you smooth out any air bubbles or creases while they are still tacky.

STEP 4 Cut out the foam board flush to the edge of the border of the image.

STEP 5 Repeat step 3 for the mirrored images, this time mounting them on the back of each relevant piece. If you have been precise, the edges should

match up, but you can always do some trimming to make them neat.

STEP 6 Find the distribution point of each bird by pinching the top loosely. Each one will balance differently depending on where you hold it, due to the different shapes. Pierce this point (not your finger!) with a needle.

STEP 7 Thread fishing wire through the hole and tie it neatly. It is easier to thread the wire through the hole by hand as opposed to using a needle, as the needle eye can get stuck.

STEP 8 How you hang your birds is up to you. You could use a chandelier for a decadent mobile; or you could create a cross strut using some twigs from your garden or local park to really get back to nature. Tie each bird to your frame, considering different hanging heights and spacing. You now have a beautiful mobile so you can birdwatch anytime – and no binoculars are required.

Here are some extremely popular tea-party offerings. These cakes are wonderfully moist, made even more heavenly by the rich chocolate butter icing. The prunes give the cakes their depth of flavour and moisture.

CHOCOLATE PRUNE tea cakes

PREP
1 hour, plus chilling
COOKING
50–60 minutes
SERVES 8

300g (10½oz) prunes, stoned

700ml (1¼ pints) weak tea

200g (7oz) plain flour

3 tbsp unsweetened cocoa powder

4 tsp baking powder

½ tsp bicarbonate of soda

250ml (9fl oz) milk

175g (6oz) butter, softened

350g (12oz) caster sugar

3 large free-range eggs

toasted almond flakes, to decorate

For the chocolate butter icing

240ml (9fl oz) double cream

115g (4oz) butter

70g (2½oz) caster sugar

¼ tsp salt

450g (1lb) dark chocolate, chopped

1 tsp vanilla extract

1 Preheat the oven to 180°C/fan 160°C/gas mark 4. Line a 23 × 33cm (9 × 13in) baking tin with nonstick baking paper. In a large pan, cover the prunes with the tea, bring to the boil and cook for 20 minutes or until the prunes are tender. If necessary, add water to keep the prunes covered. Allow to cool, drain the prunes and set aside.

2 In a medium-sized bowl, combine the flour, cocoa powder, baking powder and bicarbonate of soda. Stir well and set aside. In a separate bowl, combine the prune purée with the milk. Set aside.

3 Beat the butter and sugar until light and fluffy. Add the eggs one at a time, beating well after each addition. Beat one-third of the dry ingredients into the butter mixture, then mix in half the prune purée. Beat in another third of the dry ingredients, the rest of the prune purée and the remaining dry ingredients.

4 Pour the batter into the prepared tin. Bake for 30–40 minutes, or until a toothpick inserted into the centre emerges clean. Cool the cake in the tin for 10 minutes, then remove from the tin and place on a wire rack to cool completely. Cut into 12–16 rounds with a 5cm (2in) cutter.

5 To make the icing, combine the cream, butter, sugar and salt in a saucepan and bring to a simmer over a low heat, stirring. Remove from the heat and add the chocolate. Leave to stand for 5 minutes, then whisk in the vanilla extract.

6 Scrape the icing into a bowl and chill until it is of spreading consistency. If it becomes too firm, leave at room temperature until it softens a bit. Using a spatula, thinly coat the top and sides of each cake with the icing. Top with toasted almond flakes. Chill in the refrigerator for 15 minutes to harden.

This recipe was given to me by a dear friend when I first started Vintage Patisserie. She told me that this cake was a sure-fire hit as she had baked it for numerous school and church fairs, and it was always the first to go – and she was right. This decadent cake is a chocoholic's dream, with its rich, dense chocolatey texture. I have tinkered with the original recipe and replaced the flour with ground almonds to make it gluten free. The almonds also give it a richer taste and fudgier quality.

DeÇaDeNt GLuTeN-FRee CHoColaTe Cake

PREP
15 minutes

COOKING
35–40 minutes,
plus cooling

SERVES 10

200g (7oz) butter

200g (7oz) dark chocolate

175g (6oz) caster sugar

4 free-range eggs

2 tbsp ground almonds

1 Preheat the oven to 180°C/fan 160°C/gas mark 4. Line a 20cm (8in) round cake tin with nonstick baking paper.

2 Melt the butter with the chocolate in a bowl set over a pan of simmering water, making sure that the bottom of the bowl doesn't touch the water. Add the sugar and stir occasionally with a wooden spoon until the sugar has dissolved. Let the mixture cool a little before adding the eggs one by one, mixing well after each addition. Add the ground almonds and mix again until smooth.

3 Pour the batter into the prepared tin and bake for 20–25 minutes, until the centre is set but still a little wobbly. Turn the oven off but leave the cake inside for another 10 minutes, then remove from the oven and place the tin on a wire rack to cool completely.

4 Remove the cake from the tin, then wrap it in clingfilm and store it in the refrigerator. Take it out about 1 hour before serving. Remove from the clingfilm and serve in generous slices.

When I first started making these very moreish delights,
I couldn't stop eating them and ended up making double batches.
These days I am more controlled and only need to make an
extra half batch. They are truly delicious – rich, buttery and
chocolatey with a crisp bite. The biscuits also taste wonderful on
their own if you can't be bothered to make the chocolate filling.

CHOCOLATE MELTING MOMENTS

PREP
15 minutes,
plus setting

COOKING
25 minutes

MAKES 18

150g (5½oz) butter, diced

70g (2½oz) icing sugar, sifted

25g (1oz) cornflour

25g (1oz) cocoa powder

125g (4½oz) plain flour

For the filling

30g (1oz) dark chocolate, broken into pieces

2 tbsp double cream

sugar-coated chocolate sweets, dragées or hundreds and thousands (optional)

1 Preheat the oven to 190°C/fan 170°C/gas mark 5. Cream the butter and
icing sugar. Sift the cornflour, cocoa powder and flour together and add to
the butter-and-icing sugar mixture. You should have a soft, squidgy dough.

2 Arrange 18 paper cases inside 2 fairy-cake trays. Roll the dough into 18
walnut-sized balls and, using your finger, make a shallow dent in each one.
Place them, dent-side up, in the cases, gently pressing into place. Bake for
15–20 minutes. Transfer the trays to wire racks and cool for 5 minutes, then
remove the biscuits from the trays and allow to cool to room temperature.

3 For the filling, melt the chocolate in a bowl set over a pan of simmering
water, making sure that the bottom of the bowl doesn't touch the water.
Stir in the cream in two goes and whisk until smooth. Drop ½ teaspoon of
the chocolate cream into the middle of each cake to fill the hole. Add the
sweets, dragées or hundreds and thousands, if using. Set aside for an hour
or two for the filling to set. If you like, you can now peel off the paper. The
cakes will keep well for a couple of days in a sealed container in a cool place.

These delicious, buttery coffee biscuits are quite fun to serve with a hot drink... or a Charlie Chaplin! I like hanging the cane on the rim of the cup – just make sure that the drink isn't filled to the brim or the cane will crumble and Charlie will shout!

Black Coffee Canes

PREP
25 minutes,
plus chilling

COOKING
12–15 minutes

MAKES 16

150g (5½oz) plain flour

50g (1¾oz) cocoa powder

1 tbsp finely ground espresso beans

225g (8oz) butter

60g (2¼oz) icing sugar

1 tsp vanilla extract

100g (3½oz) white chocolate

1 Preheat the oven to 180°C/fan 160°C/gas mark 4, with two racks spaced evenly apart. Line two baking sheets with nonstick baking paper.

2 Sift together the flour, cocoa powder and ground espresso beans into a medium bowl. Set aside.

3 In the bowl of an electric mixer fitted with a paddle attachment, combine the butter, icing sugar and vanilla extract. Beat on a medium setting until creamy (about 3–4 minutes). Reduce the speed to low and gradually beat in the flour mixture, scraping down the sides of the bowl twice.

4 Fit a piping bag with a plain round nozzle and fill it with the mixture. Pipe in equal lengths, about 10–13cm (4–5in), on to a prepared baking sheet. While still soft, bend the ends of each pipe into a cane shape. Chill in the freezer for about 5 minutes.

5 Bake the canes for 12–15 minutes or until just firm to the touch. Transfer to a wire rack to cool.

6 Melt the white chocolate in a bowl set over a saucepan of simmering water, making sure that the base of the bowl does not touch the water. Remove the chocolate from the heat, allow it to cool slightly, then transfer it to a disposable piping bag. Cut a tiny hole at the bag's point and decorate the canes with the melted chocolate.

Tarts are so versatile, and if you use ready-made shortcrust pastry (choose the all-butter type, if possible) they are super quick to make as well. You can fill them with anything you like: caramel, bananas and whipped cream; little balls of ice cream and chopped nuts; or, my favourite, cream cheese mixed with a bit of honey and cream and topped with a raspberry. Delicious!

MINI TARTS FILLED WITH DELICIOUSNESS

PREP
25 minutes,
plus chilling
and cooling

COOKING
15 minutes

MAKES 24

125g (4½oz) plain flour

40g (1½oz) icing sugar

½ tsp salt

115g (4oz) chilled butter, cut into pieces

2 free-range egg yolks, lightly beaten with 1 tbsp water

Orange and Lemon Curd (*see* page 84), Chocolate Butter Icing (*see* page 151), or fruit and cream, to fill

1 Combine the flour, icing sugar and salt in the bowl of a food processor and pulse once to mix. Add the butter and pulse for 20–25 seconds, until the mixture forms pea-sized crumbs. While pulsing, add the egg yolk mixture and process for 10–15 seconds more, until large, moist crumbs form. Turn the pastry out on to a lightly floured surface, shape it into a ball and divide it in half. Press each half into a flat, 12.5cm (4¾in) disc, cover with clingfilm and refrigerate for at least 1 hour.

2 Preheat the oven to 200ºC/fan 180°C/gas mark 6. Working with one piece of pastry at a time, roll out to 5mm (¼in) thickness. Using a 7.5cm (3in) round shape cutter, cut out 12 rounds. Press a round into each well of a 12-hole mini-muffin tin. Repeat this process with the second half of the pastry.

3 Bake for 15 minutes, until the tart shells are evenly golden and crisp. Transfer the tin to a wire rack and cool for 5 minutes, then remove the tart shells from the tin and allow to cool to room temperature. To serve, fill each tart shell with 1½ tablespoons of your chosen filling.

A good meringue is crisp on the outside and chewy on the inside. Meringues are simple to make when you know how: the trick is to cook them slowly at a low temperature. Sandwich them around a dollop of whipped cream, then drizzle over some chocolate sauce and you have an instant dessert. They taste equally good crushed with a mixture of cream and Greek yogurt with fresh fruit. You can keep them in an airtight tin for up to two weeks, or store them in the freezer for a standby pudding.

CANDY-STRIPED MERINGUES

PREP
40 minutes

COOKING
40 minutes

MAKES 30

4 free-range egg whites
225g (8oz) icing sugar, sifted
3 drops of vanilla extract
few drops each of black and red food colouring

1 Preheat the oven to 140°C/fan 120°C/gas mark 1 and line a couple of baking sheets with nonstick baking paper.

2 Whisk the egg whites and icing sugar until the mixture is thick and will form firm peaks. Add the vanilla extract and whisk for a further 2 minutes.

3 Using a small paintbrush, straw or the handle of a spoon, paint 2 or 3 stripes of black food colouring on the inside of a piping bag.

4 Fit the piping bag with a star-shaped nozzle and spoon half the meringue mixture into the bag. Pipe small 2cm (¾in) high star shapes on to the prepared baking sheets. Repeat steps 3 and 4 with red food colouring and the remaining meringue mixture.

5 Bake the meringues for 40 minutes, until they are crisp but not brown. Turn off the oven and leave the meringues to cool inside overnight, with the oven door slightly ajar, to ensure that the outsides are crispy and the insides are soft and chewy.

FLAG HISTORY

I'm British
and I'm very proud of it.

Our history, our royal family, our castles and stately
homes, our pearly queens, our fish and chips, our Sunday
roast, our high tea, our cheese, our strawberries, our tennis... even
our infamous rain – I embrace them all. But what could be more iconic
than the Union Jack?

The Union Flag, or Union Jack as it's more commonly known, was created in 1606 by
King James VI of Scotland, who became King James I when Queen Elizabeth I died. He
wanted a flag that represented both his kingdoms, so he combined the red cross of England
with the saltire of Scotland. A white border was added around the red cross because the rules
of heraldry state that colours (such as red and blue) cannot touch. The flag was to be used purely
on the King's ships while the original flags of England and Scotland were to be used on land.
However this changed in 1707 when Queen Anne proclaimed the flag as the national flag of Great
Britain and allowed its use on land and at sea.

When Ireland was unified with Great Britain in 1801 the flag had to be redesigned, so the red cross
of St Patrick was added to it. And here's an interesting fact: many people think that the Union
Jack is symmetrical – but look closely and you will find that it's not. The rules of heraldry are
quite complicated but, in a nutshell, as Scotland had joined the Union nearly 200 years earlier
than Ireland, its flag was placed in the most honoured position, the top quarter nearest the
flagstaff. The Irish cross had the second most honoured position – the top quarter of the fly.

I used to wonder why the Welsh flag was not included in the Union Jack, but then my
history teacher explained that Wales was already united with England back in the
13th century so, in effect, it was already represented.

So take care when flying the Union Jack because you may accidentally hang
it upside down. To do so could mean one of two things: it could be a signal
for help (it is very rarely used for this purpose, but the troops in
the Boer War and some campaigns in India in the 19th century
did just that), or it could be done as an insult to the
crown, which is described by the French term
lèse majesté, which means, literally,
'injured majesty'.

QUEEN ELIZABETH
STENCIL

YOU WILL NEED

access to a photocopier ✄ paper ✄ Queen Elizabeth stencil (*see* previous page) ✄ craft knife ✄ cutting mat ✄ your handmade flag (*see* instructions on pages 163–167) ✄ sticky tape ✄ acrylic paint (whatever colour you want) ✄ screen-printing medium (available from craft shops) ✄ piece of card (approximately the width of the stencil) ✄ iron ✄ ironing board

STEP 1 Photocopy the Queen Elizabeth stencil on page 161 and cut out the black areas carefully using a craft knife and a cutting mat.

STEP 2 Lay out your flag on a flat surface and place the stencil in the desired position. Tape down the corners so that it won't move around.

STEP 3 Mix up your paint and medium in 50:50 ratio. Make sure it's thoroughly mixed, or the thickness of the mixture will vary.

STEP 4 Using the piece of card, put some of the paint on to the bottom of the stencil in a fairly even stripe; this will make it easier to scrape.

STEP 5 In one fluid motion, scrape all the paint upwards so that it fills all the negative stencil space. Try not to scrape the paint too thickly as it will not dry evenly and may bleed over the stencil edges.

STEP 6 Leave for about a minute and then carefully peel off the stencil. Leave the flag to dry overnight. If you want to seal the paint permanently, you can iron it when it's completely dry, which will also get rid of any creases.

FLAG MAKING

YOU WILL NEED

scissors ✄ paper ✄ red, white and blue cotton or muslin ✄
pins ✄ iron-on Vilene ✄ iron ✄ ironing board ✄ sewing
machine ✄ white or cream thread ✄ kettle ✄ 3 tea bags
✄ bowl ✄ wooden pole ✄ staple gun

STEP 1 Cut out paper pattern pieces using the template on pages 166–167.

STEP 2 Match these to the correct coloured fabric, pin to secure and carefully cut out.

STEP 3 Cut a piece of Vilene roughly the size of the finished flag.

STEP 4 Lay the Vilene out and place the top and bottom, left and right small white strips on, leaving about a 5cm (2in) gap between each strip (this is where the central red strips will be placed later).

STEP 5 Next, lay the top and bottom, left and right long white strips in place, overlapping slightly the small white pieces which are already in place.

STEP 6 When the white strips are in place, the central red strips can be positioned. Start with the central left and right pieces, making sure they slightly overlap the white edges.

STEP 7 Next lay the central red strip in place, making sure the edges overlap any white or red strips already in place so that it all looks neat and tidy. (Continued on page 165.)

STEP 8 Once the central strips are in place, the corners can be assembled. Starting with the top left corner, lay the two white strips (4 and 2) on to the Vilene backing first, lining them up with the sides that are already in place; at this stage the edges of the corner strips are going to overlap the central white strips.

STEP 9 Once in place, lay the red strip (3) overlapping both the white pieces either side of it.

STEP 10 Finally, lay the two blue triangles (1 and 5) at either corner of the square, making sure the edges of the blue slightly overlap each white edge.

STEP 11 Once you're satisfied that all your strips look as if they are in the correct place, then this process can be carried out on every corner square until all pieces are in place.

STEP 12 When all the corner pieces are in place, the edges that will be overlapping the central white lines need to be tucked underneath, so that the central white lines are overlapping all the corner strips to make it look neat.

STEP 13 Once all is in place, very carefully move your flag over to the ironing board (or even assemble it there). Cover with a piece of paper and iron the pieces down on a medium heat setting, so the glue on the Vilene will set the pieces in place.

STEP 14 After ironing, use a straight stitch on your sewing machine to stitch around the strips to ensure all stay securely in place. You won't need to sew around every strip, because you have overlapped them, so just make sure when you stitch that everything is secured.

STEP 15 Once sewn, it's time to dye your flag. Boil about 1 litre (1¾ pints) water in the kettle and pour it over 3 tea bags in a bowl. Wet your flag and then lay it in the tea water, giving it a good stir to make sure the whole flag is covered. Leave for about 15 minutes.

STEP 16 After soaking, take out your flag, give it a rinse in cold water and leave it to dry.

STEP 17 If you want a double-sided flag, repeat the procedure so that you have two flags. When complete, make sure they are the right way up and sew them back to back.

STEP 18 Once dry, the flag will need a bit of a press to remove any creases. Then you can attach it to the pole. Using a staple gun, staple the edge of the flag to the wooden pole, keeping it securely in place.

STEP 19 It's important to make sure that your flag is the correct way up when attaching it to the post (see page 160).

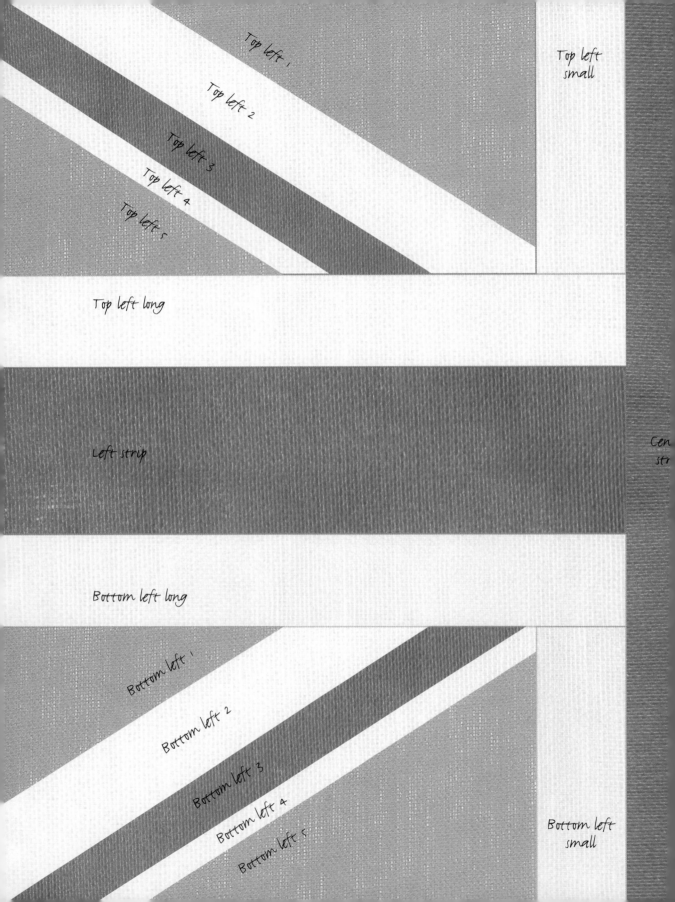

Top left 1

Top left 2

Top left 3

Top left 4

Top left 5

Top left
small

Top left long

Left strip

Cen
str

Bottom left long

Bottom left 1

Bottom left 2

Bottom left 3

Bottom left 4

Bottom left 5

Bottom left
small

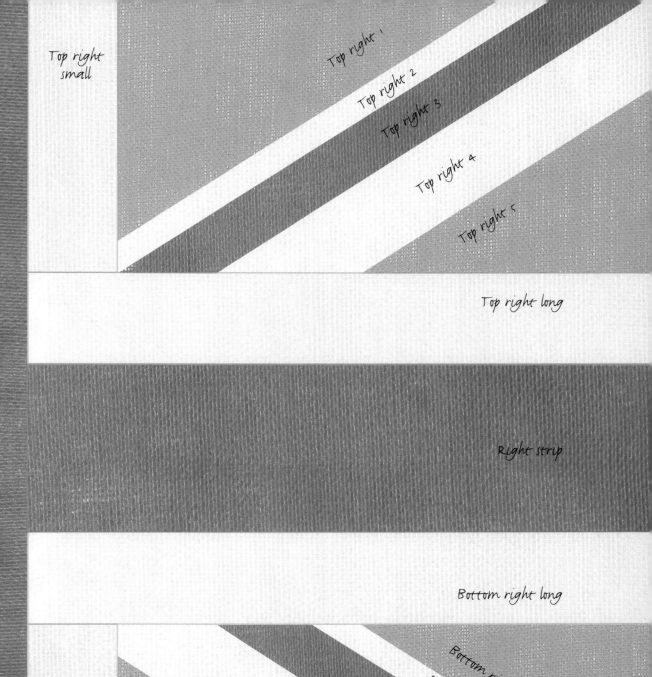

Top right
small

Top right 1

Top right 2

Top right 3

Top right 4

Top right 5

Top right long

Right strip

Bottom right long

Bottom right 1

Bottom right 2

Bottom right 3

Bottom right 4

Bottom
right small

Bottom right 5

I'm convinced that if I were to do a survey asking 100 people to name a dessert most reminiscent of childhood times, jelly would feature highly. Some may consider that it should be left in the realm of nostalgic memories... but I disagree. Jellies are a great way to add some fun and colour to any afternoon tea party. And the people who at first turn their noses up are often the ones going back for second helpings. It's great to add alcohol and fruit, so be as creative as you want.

ANiMaL Jellies

PREP
25 minutes,
plus chilling
SERVES 6

4 tbsp water

1 sachet or 3 tsp powdered gelatine

40g (1½oz) caster sugar

For the tortoise

500ml (18fl oz) rosé wine

250g (9oz) small strawberries, hulled and halved

For the rabbit

500ml (18fl oz) Sauternes or other dessert wine

250g (9oz) mixed blackberries and black grapes, deseeded

1 Put the water in a small heatproof bowl, then sprinkle the gelatine over the top, so that it is completely absorbed. Leave to soak for 5 minutes, then set the bowl over a small saucepan of simmering water for 5 minutes or until a clear liquid forms. Remove from the heat, then stir in the sugar until it dissolves. Allow to cool slightly, then gradually mix in the wine.

2 Place the fruits in a 600ml (1 pint) jelly mould. Pour the jelly mixture over them, cover with clingfilm and refrigerate for about 3 hours until firmly set.

3 Run the tip of a small pointed knife around the top edge of the mould to loosen the jelly. Fill a large bowl with warm water and dip the jelly mould into the water just to the rim for about 10 seconds. Place a plate on top of the mould and, keeping it firmly in place, invert both the plate and the mould. Give the mould a shake, still holding the plate in place, then carefully lift it off. If the jelly doesn't release, dip the mould in water again.

These are so pretty that whenever I serve them I'm greeted by ooohs and aaahs, and people often tell me that they don't have the heart to eat them. But they would be missing out on a treat, as these silky milky delights are lightly scented with rose essence and taste as good as they look.

Rose Pannacotta

PREP
25–30 minutes,
plus chilling

COOKING
10 minutes

SERVES 6

6 tbsp water

6 tsp powdered gelatine

350ml (12fl oz) milk

700ml (1¼ pints) double cream

950g (2lb 2oz) caster sugar

½ tsp rose-petal essence

6 edible rose transfers (available online)

1 Put the water in a small heatproof bowl, then sprinkle the gelatine over the top. Leave to soak for 5 minutes, then set the bowl over a small saucepan of simmering water for 5 minutes or until a clear liquid forms. Set aside.

2 Place the milk, cream and sugar in a large saucepan and heat, stirring constantly. When at boiling point, remove from the heat, add the rose-petal essence and gelatine liquid, and stir. Divide this mixture between 6 dariole moulds, ramekin dishes or teacups and refrigerate for about 3 hours until firmly set (it shouldn't sag when you tilt the mould).

3 Run the tip of a small pointed knife around the top edge of the moulds to loosen them. Next, fill a large bowl with hot water and dip the moulds into the water just to the rim for about 10 seconds. Place a plate on top of each mould and, keeping it firmly in place, invert the plate and the mould at the same time. Give the mould a shake, still holding the plate in place underneath it, then lift the mould off carefully. If the pannacotta doesn't release easily, dip the mould in water again.

4 Before serving, apply a rose transfer to the top of each pannacotta, holding each transfer in place for at least 30 seconds and delicately rubbing the reverse side to ensure that the image transfers.

I'm an old-fashioned girl at heart and I love traditional desserts. Trifle is one of my favourites – the cake, the booze, some jelly, custard and cream… what a wonderful concoction of ingredients. It's also really quick to make if you use packet jelly.

CHERRY AND DARK CHOCOLATE TRIFLE SHOTS

PREP
25 minutes
SERVES 6

6 sponge fingers, broken into small pieces

100ml (3½fl oz) cherry brandy or chocolate liqueur

50g (1¾oz) dark chocolate, grated

1 pack of dark cherry jelly (made and set according to the instructions on the pack, then chopped up and bashed a bit)

jar of morello cherries

100ml (3½fl oz) custard

100ml (3½fl oz) whipped cream

1 Arrange the sponge finger pieces at the bottom of 6 shot glasses. Add 1 tablespoon of your chosen liqueur to each one and sprinkle with 1 teaspoon of grated chocolate.

2 Once the sponge fingers have absorbed the liqueur, add a heaped tablespoon of prepared jelly to each shot, then top with a few cherries and more grated chocolate.

3 To serve, top each shot with a heaped tablespoon of custard and a generous tablespoon of whipped cream, and finish with the obligatory decorative sprinkle of grated chocolate.

We all need a bit of 'bling' in our lives, but if you can't afford
the real thing (who can these days?) you can just make
some, admire (or wear if you dare), then eat them.
I like pairing flavours and colours such
as pink with rose flavouring, green with
peppermint, yellow with lemon... you get
the picture. Now, smile for the camera!

EDIBLE JEWEL SWEETS

PREP
25 minutes,
plus cooling

MAKES 30

85ml (3fl oz) corn syrup

225g (8oz) caster sugar

½ tsp flavouring of
your choice, such as
peppermint, vanilla,
strawberry or orange

2–3 drops of liquid food colouring

1 Place the corn syrup, sugar and 250ml (9fl oz) water in a small saucepan and bring to the boil over a medium–high heat. Continue to heat until the temperature of the syrup reaches 150°C on a sugar thermometer, then remove from the heat.

2 Using a rubber spatula, stir the flavouring and food colouring into the syrup – the mixture will bubble and steam at this stage, so take care. Transfer to a measuring jug and allow the bubbles to settle for about 15 seconds.

3 Carefully pour the mixture into two silicone gem sweet mould trays (heat-resistant moulds designed for sugar work that can be ordered online). Set aside to cool for about 30 minutes or until the sweets harden. Remove the sweets from the moulds to serve.

Every Christmas, from the age of five to at least my early teens, I'd make floral creams with my gran to give as gifts. I remember being impressed at how easy it was to create something so yummy and elegant. The mint creams are great at the end of a tea party and I'm a huge fan of the rose-scented creams, too.

Floral Creams

PREP
25 minutes,
plus chilling

MAKES 20

45ml (1½fl oz) double cream

1 drop of food colouring of your choice

45ml (1½fl oz) rose, violet, mint or lavender syrup (available online)

275g (9¾oz) icing sugar, plus extra for dusting

100g (3½oz) dark chocolate, broken into pieces

1 tsp sunflower oil

20 edible sugared rose or violet petals, sugared mint leaf pieces or lavender florets, to decorate (available online)

1 Place the cream, food colouring and syrup in a bowl and mix well. Sift the icing sugar over the cream mixture and stir to combine.

2 Dust a work surface lightly with icing sugar, then tip the cream mixture out on to it and knead with your hands until it comes together in a firm ball. Wrap in clingfilm and place in the refrigerator for about 30 minutes. Remove the fondant from the refrigerator and unwrap it. Divide it into 20 teaspoon-sized lumps, roll them into balls and place on a plate. Set aside.

3 Melt the dark chocolate in a bowl set over a saucepan of simmering water, ensuring the base of the bowl does not touch the water. Stir in the sunflower oil, then remove the chocolate from the heat. Allow to cool for around 10 minutes.

4 Meanwhile, line a 39 × 35cm (15½ × 14in) baking sheet with nonstick baking paper. Working quickly, dip the fondant balls halfway into the melted chocolate one at a time. Place each coated ball carefully on to the nonstick baking paper. Top each with an edible sugared petal or leaf and set aside to harden in the refrigerator for 15 minutes. Serve as they are, or in individual petit-four cases, if you wish.

The pleasure of receiving a gift that has been handmade with love and care outweighs that of receiving a shop-bought present any day. People's time is priceless and giving a delicious gift such as this one gives the impression that you have spent a good amount of time slaving away to achieve taste and perfection.

engraved EARL GREY TRUFFLE hearts

PREP
10 minutes,
plus chilling

MAKES
about 25

125g (4½oz) chocolate
(I use a mixture of half dark and half milk)
100g (3½oz) extra-thick cream
2 tsp loose Earl Grey tea

1 Cut the chocolate into pieces that are as small as you can make them. Place them in a bowl ready for the hot cream to be poured on to them.

2 Heat the cream and the tea in a pan over a low heat to infuse the flavour. When the mixture starts to boil, remove from the heat and pour through a strainer on to the chocolate.

3 Leave for a couple of minutes to ensure the chocolate has melted, then mix into a silky consistency (this mixture is called a ganache). Line a baking sheet with nonstick baking paper, then pour the ganache on to it. I start in the middle and spread the mixture with a spatula, trying for an even coverage of around 15mm (⅝in) thickness.

4 Pop the ganache into the refrigerator for a couple of hours until set. Now use a shape cutter to create your truffles – you can buy a huge variety on the trusty internet or in good cookshops. I also stamp the truffles with an unused ink-stamp to mark friends' names and the dates of events – a personal touch that helps make a tea party extra memorable.

It might seem a bit odd to serve a soup for dessert, but this one is really good. It's a lovely blend of flavours and the crème fraîche gives it a velvety texture. This refreshing dish could even be offered as a starter (as they do in Scandinavian countries) on a hot summer's day.

CHILLED RASPBERRY SOUP

PREP
10 minutes,
plus chilling

SERVES 4

50ml (2fl oz) cranberry juice

50g (1¾oz) caster sugar

400g (14oz) raspberries, plus extra to decorate

100ml (3½fl oz) crème fraîche,
plus extra to decorate

4 sprigs of mint, to decorate

1 In a blender, combine the cranberry juice, sugar and raspberries. Cover and process until blended, then strain. Tap the side of the sieve to ensure the maximum amount of juice comes through, then discard the raspberry seeds. Stir the crème fraîche into the purée. Cover and refrigerate for at least 2 hours.

2 To serve, pour into bowls and top each one with a swirl of crème fraîche, a raspberry and a sprig of mint.

This delightful combination of orange, lemon and lemongrass makes a fantastic change from ordinary lemonade. The beautiful muted pink colour from the blood orange is a happy bonus. If you can't get hold of blood oranges, then normal oranges will work just as well.

Punch ignites some interesting memories for me... my friends still talk about the punch bowl I had at my 21st birthday party! Here I've made it clean, healthy and visually striking. The ice ring really lifts this punch. It stays solid for hours, too, so you can top it up with delicious juices and it remains cold.

bLOOD ORANGE LEMONADE

PREP
25 minutes,
plus chilling

COOKING
30 minutes

SERVES 6–8

70g (2½oz) caster sugar

600ml (1 pint) water

2 lemongrass stalks

grated rind of 2 blood oranges (or a citrus fruit of your choice, such as grapefruit, lemon or orange)

juice of 6 blood oranges (or a citrus fruit of your choice – see suggestions above)

juice of 2 lemons (or a citrus fruit of your choice – see suggestions above)

soda water

1 Place the sugar in a saucepan with the water over a medium heat.

2 Bash the lemongrass to release the flavour and add this to the pan. Bring the water to the boil and then reduce the heat to low. Stir until the sugar has dissolved and the mixture becomes syrupy.

3 Remove the syrup from the heat and place in the refrigerator to chill. When cooled, strain into a jug, add the grated rind and juice and top off with the soda water.

SUNSHINE PUNCH

PREP
10–15 minutes,
plus freezing

SERVES 18

8 maraschino cherries

1 orange, thinly sliced and the slices cut into quarters

1 small lemon, thinly sliced

1 small lime, thinly sliced

75ml (2½fl oz) elderflower cordial

500ml (18fl oz) pineapple juice, chilled

500ml (18fl oz) orange juice, chilled

2 litres (3½ pints) ginger ale, chilled

1 Arrange the fruit in a ring mould and add just enough water to cover the fruit (too much water and the fruit may float away).

2 Freeze for 2 hours until the contents are solid, then add enough water to fill the mould entirely. Return to the freezer for another 3 hours, until solid.

3 Just before serving, take the ring mould out of the freezer and remove the ice ring by running the bottom of the mould under a cold tap. Invert the mould on to a clean plate, then slide the ice ring into a large punch bowl, fruit side up. Combine the cordial and juices and pour over the ice ring. Finally add the ginger ale and serve immediately.

SUNSHINE PUNCH

This is simplicity at its best – just mangoes, mint and bubbly. It's great on both the taste buds and the eye as the mint adds a refreshing zing and the mango lends a gleaming golden hue to the drink. Experiment with other fruits: pomegranate and blueberries add a beautiful vibrant purple hue to the Champagne, while strawberries produce a delicate pink tone.

MaNGo and MiNT ice cubes for bellinis

PREP
20–25 minutes,
plus freezing

MAKES 12

2 mangoes, or about 150ml (5fl oz) mango juice

12 mint leaves

ice bowl, to serve

2 bottles of Champagne or dry, sparkling white wine, chilled

1 If using fresh mangoes, remove the skin and stones, chop the flesh roughly, then blend it to a purée in a food processor. Divide the purée between the 12 cups of an ice-cube tray. If using juice, just pour this into the ice-cube tray.

2 Place the tray in the freezer for 45 minutes, until the cubes are semi-frozen, then remove. Place a small mint leaf on top of each cube, taking care to ensure that it is centred. Return the tray to the freezer until the juice is frozen solid.

3 To make the ice bowl, place two small plastic or metal bowls one inside the other (the space between the bowls will be the size and thickness of your eventual ice bowl) and place a weight inside the inner bowl. Fill the outer bowl with water, then place the bowls in the freezer. Once the water has frozen, remove the inner bowl, then turn the ice bowl out on to a clean surface. If you have trouble removing the ice from the bowl, dip the bottom of it in warm water for a few seconds to loosen.

4 Present the ice cubes in the ice bowl. To serve the drinks, place an ice cube in the bottom of each of 12 Champagne glasses and top up with Champagne or sparkling white wine. Serve immediately.

They say that the first bite is with the eye. Somewhere deep down inside I have always been aware of this concept. As a child I would always chose a red or orange slush drink because the thought of having something blue that was apparently raspberry-flavoured horrified me. Slushes are a real treat on a hot summer's day, and they are incredibly easy to make. Freeze any drink you want for up to 4 hours, depending on the alcohol content, then stir and serve immediately. The recipes below are designed to inspire you and help you on your way. The warmth of the bourbon or brandy provides a great contrast to the iciness of the slush.

BOURBON SLUSH

PREP
5 minutes, plus
chilling and
freezing

SERVES 6

12 English Breakfast tea bags
300ml (½ pint) just-boiled water
100g (3½oz) caster sugar,
or to taste
100ml (3½fl oz) bourbon
850ml (1½ pints) lemonade
strips of lemon rind, to serve

1 Steep the tea bags in the water in a measuring jug for 3 minutes, adding the sugar and stirring until dissolved. Remove the tea bags.

2 Chill the tea in the refrigerator for 30 minutes.

3 Add the bourbon and lemonade, then place the mixture in the freezer for up to 4 hours or until it reaches a slushy consistency (the timing depends on how powerful your freezer is).

4 Remove the slush from freezer, stir, then divide between 6 short glasses and serve decorated with a strip of lemon rind.

BRANDY AND GREEN TEA SLUSH

PREP
5 minutes, plus
chilling and
freezing

SERVES 6

12 green tea bags
300ml (½ pint) just-boiled water
100g (3½oz) caster sugar, or to taste
100ml (3½fl oz) brandy
850ml (1½ pints) ginger ale
strips of orange rind, to serve

1 Steep the tea bags in the water in a measuring jug for 3 minutes, adding the sugar and stirring until dissolved. Remove the tea bags.

2 Chill the tea in the refrigerator for 30 minutes.

3 Add the brandy and ginger ale, then place the mixture in the freezer for up to 4 hours or until the mixture reaches a slushy consistency (the timing depends on how powerful your freezer is).

4 Remove the slush from freezer, stir, then divide between 6 short glasses and serve decorated with strips of orange rind.

EVENING

Evening Contents

Shower your guests with glamour, decadence and indulgence. Woo them with the romance and mystery of the evening that lies ahead of you all.

An evening tea party does not follow tradition, so allow yourself to be inspired by this chapter and be as free and innovative as you possibly can.

Be warned, you may find yourself repeating the following:

'Why thank you. It's incredibly easy to make.'

'Why thank you. I picked it up in a charity shop and thought it would make the perfect table decoration.'

'Why thank you. I tried my hardest to look fabulous.'

All that's left to do is dance, laugh, get merry and watch the sun come up.

Brunch, anyone?

Mmm! There's nothing more decadent than having a tray of luscious juicy oysters to feast on. The runny salty juices and the soft tender bite of the oyster with its briny, tangy flavours – it's an all-time favourite of mine. I also live in hope that maybe one day I might find a pearl in one of these beauties. To add a bit more glitz and glamour to this luxurious treat, why not sprinkle on some real gold? You might not be able to taste it, but it sure makes the dish look spectacular.

24-Carat Oysters

PREP
15 minutes
SERVES 6

12 oysters

1 tsp cayenne pepper

1 sheet of edible gold leaf (available from most good cake shops or the internet)

plenty of rock salt

12 lemon wedges

1 To open an oyster, hold it down firmly with a tea towel and, using an oyster knife, prise it open at the hinge, twisting if you need to. When it opens, slide the knife between the two shell halves and work your way round, easing them apart. Remove the 'lid', being careful not to lose any of the juices.

2 Now slide the knife underneath the oyster so that it is completely separated from the shell (but still sitting in it) and will slip out easily when tipped into the mouth.

3 Sprinkle a pinch of cayenne pepper over each oyster in the shell.

4 To make gold flakes, use tweezers to break off tiny pieces from the sheet and put them in a small bowl. Sprinkle 4–6 flakes over each oyster.

5 Arrange the oysters in their shells on a cake stand or serving dish. (If you cover the plate with rock salt first, it will stop the oysters sliding around.) Serve each oyster with a wedge of lemon for squeezing just before you eat.

6 To eat, hold the shell with the shallower end towards you. Tip the shell back so that the oyster slides directly into your mouth.

Potting is a traditional British method for preserving foods. This method was particularly popular during World war II but, like all things old and wonderful, its making a comeback! And this party entree is too easy for words. It looks super stylish and tastes divine. The butter not only gives this dish a rich flavour, but also acts as a preservative to allow it to stay fresh for up to four weeks in the refrigerator (not that it will last that long!).

POTTED PRAWNS SPRINKLED WITH PORK SCRATCHINGS

PREP
10 minutes
SERVES 6

250g (9oz) butter
400g (14oz) small cooked prawns, at room temperature
1 tsp cayenne pepper
½ tsp ground nutmeg
pinch of sea salt
black pepper

To serve
1 bag of pork scratchings, approximately 90g (3¼oz)
6 large cooked prawns, with shells on
6 slices of Melba Toast (*see* page 72)

1 Melt the butter in a small pan and use a large spoon to skim off the white solids on the surface. Pour the clarified butter into a bowl, then add the small prawns, spices and seasoning and mix well. Spoon into 6 small pots or glasses.

2 For a cheeky topping, sprinkle over a few pieces of pork scratchings. Separate the legs on the shell-on prawns so that they can 'sit' on the side of the glasses. Serve with warm Melba Toast.

Choux pastry is light and airy, and cooks with a crisp yet soft shell, a moist lining and a hollow centre, which is perfect for filling with either sweet or savoury goodies. Here, these dinky little buns are filled with a moreish crab mixture. Once, when I made them for an evening event, nearly every guest asked for more, so it might be worth making double quantities.

crab CHOUX

PREP
45 minutes

COOKING
30 minutes

MAKES 12

For the pastry

70g (2½oz) butter

125ml (4fl oz) water

70g (2½oz) flour

2 free-range eggs, beaten

For the filling

150g (5½oz) mixed crab meat

70ml (2½fl oz) crème fraîche

3 spring onions, finely chopped

pinch of cayenne pepper

salt and black pepper

few spring onions, to garnish

1 Preheat the oven to 220°C/fan 200°C/gas mark 7. Line a baking sheet with nonstick baking paper.

2 Melt the butter in the water in a small pan over a medium heat and bring to a full boil. Immediately add all the flour in one go and stir continuously with a wooden spoon. Cook for a couple of minutes, until the mixture pulls away from the pan, forming a ball. Remove from the heat and continue stirring for 1 minute while the mixture cools down a little.

3 Gradually add the egg, mixing the dough until it is smooth each time. Scrape down the sides and bottom of the bowl until all the egg is incorporated.

4 Pipe or place 12 spoonfuls of dough, about 2.5cm (1in) in diameter, on to the prepared baking sheet. Bake for 25 minutes, until the pastry balls have risen and are golden brown.

5 To make the filling, place all the ingredients in a bowl and mix with a spoon to combine. Using a knife, make a small slit in each of the pastry balls and carefully pull the pastry apart with your hands to make a hole. Spoon or pipe a heaped teaspoonful of the filling into each ball.

6 For decoration, slice thin strips of spring onion lengthways and chill them in some ice-cold water until they curl. Sprinkle over the crab balls and serve cold.

Once upon a time, the only way to get your hands on sea trout was to dress up in a sou'wester and head out in a fishing boat. Today you just dress up and head down to your local fishmonger. Even supermarkets sell trout now. It's worth spending a bit extra on wild sea trout rather than farmed rainbow trout, because it has better colour, flavour and texture.

Trout Tartare

PREP
30 minutes,
plus chilling

SERVES 4

600g (1lb 5oz) sea trout or organic salmon fillet, finely diced

juice and grated rind of 2 juicy limes

20cm (8in) peeled cucumber, halved, seeds scooped out and flesh finely diced

4 tbsp finely chopped dill, plus extra to garnish

olive oil

salt and black pepper

For the wasabi mayonnaise (optional)

5g (⅛oz) wasabi powder

1 tsp cold water

250g (9oz) mayonnaise

1 Put the fish in a mixing bowl and pour the lime juice and rind over it. Add the cucumber, dill and approximately the same amount of olive oil as there was lime juice. Season to taste with salt and pepper and mix well.

2 Line 4 dariole moulds with clingfilm and divide the mixture between them, packing it in tightly. Transfer to the refrigerator and chill for 2 hours.

3 If you're making the Wasabi Mayonnaise, mix the wasabi powder and water together thoroughly in a small bowl to form a smooth paste, then combine with the mayonnaise. Set aside.

4 Remove the dariole moulds from the refrigerator and turn the tartares out on to individual serving plates.

5 Garnish with dill and serve with wasabi mayonnaise, if liked.

Imagine arriving at your party destination and walking into a room that's filled with romantic clusters of fluttering candles. You don't know what the evening has in store but you can't wait to find out. Getting the lighting right is key to creating the desired atmosphere. Candles are perfect for this, and they are easy to make. You can use your candleholder again and again.

YOU WILL NEED

wick tab (or metal weight) ✄ wick ✄ teacups, sugar bowls, jam jars ✄ glue dots ✄ pencil ✄ candle-making wax ✄ saucepan

STEP 1 Attach the wick tab (or metal weight) to the wick before securing it to the bottom of your cup, bowl or jar using a glue dot. Make sure that it is central.

STEP 2 Balance a pencil across the rim of the container and tie the wick to it, ensuring it is taut. This will keep the wick secure and central.

STEP 3 Break your wax into pieces and melt it in a saucepan over a very low heat. Don't leave the wax unattended at any time.

STEP 4 Pour the wax into the container, being careful not to knock the wick. Any leftover wax should be disposed of in old paper or rags, not down the kitchen sink as it will create a nasty blockage.

STEP 5 Leave the wax to cool and set completely before removing the pencil and trimming the wick.

STEP 6 Voilà! Your bespoke candle is ready.

CANDLE MAKING

When my grandmother made chopped liver, the rest of the family would vigorously fight over who got to take the leftovers home. This recipe is a little more refined, but it's a great crowd-pleaser and always one of the first platters at my parties to be polished off. The guests love the pairing of silky smooth parfait with crispy filo pastry. The little baskets look stunning, too.

CHICKEN LIVER PARFAIT
IN A FILO PASTRY BASKET

PREP
40 minutes

COOKING
12–15 minutes

MAKES 24

175g (6oz) butter

1kg (2lb 4oz) chicken livers, cleaned

50ml (2fl oz) brandy

4 tbsp double cream

salt and black pepper

8 sheets of ready-rolled filo pastry

24 pearl onions

1 Preheat the oven to 220°C/fan 200°C/gas mark 7. Heat 50g (1¾oz) of the butter in a frying pan until very hot. Add the chicken livers and cook for 3–4 minutes, turning occasionally so they cook evenly but are still pink in the middle. Add the brandy and cook until the alcohol has evaporated. Take off the heat and allow the livers to cool slightly. In a clean pan, melt another 50g (1¾oz) of the butter, then blend it with the chicken livers in a food processor. Add the cream and blend to incorporate. Season and set aside.

2 Melt the remaining butter. Using a pastry brush, brush one side of the first sheet of pastry with butter, then top with a second sheet. Butter this sheet and top with a third. Butter this and finish with a fourth (butter this too). Cut out 12 layered pastry circles with an 8cm (3¼in) pastry cutter and press these into a 12-hole mini-muffin pan. Repeat with the remaining 4 sheets of pastry. Bake the pastry baskets for 6 minutes, or until golden.

3 Remove from the pan and cool on a wire rack. Transfer the parfait to a piping bag fitted with a star-shaped nozzle and pipe into the baskets. Decorate each with a pearl onion.

In the past I've steered away from veal because of the controversy surrounding rearing practices, but since the introduction of higher welfare standards I now feel comfortable to buy it again (ask your butcher for rose veal or young beef). Veal is meltingly tender with a delicate flavour, so it goes well with sun-dried tomato tapenade. This dish is a handy dinner-party starter as you can make the roulade up to a day early and leave it in the refrigerator until 10 minutes before you're ready to serve.

Veal Roulade

PREP
30 minutes,
plus chilling

COOKING
15–20 minutes

MAKES 16–20
DISCS

4 pieces veal escalope, approximately 150g (5½oz) each

100g (3½oz) French beans

4–8 slices prosciutto, depending on size

4 tbsp sun-dried tomato tapenade from a jar

salt and black pepper

olive oil, to drizzle

1 Place each piece of veal between two sheets of clingfilm and flatten with a rolling pin until about 2mm (1/16 in) thick.

2 Blanch the French beans by dropping them in a pan of boiling water for 2 minutes. Drain and then cool under running water.

3 Place 1–2 prosciutto slices on a new piece of clingfilm. Lay one of the flattened veal escalopes on top and spread 1 tablespoon of sun-dried tomato tapenade across the veal. Arrange one-quarter of the blanched beans neatly on top of one end of the veal. Season well. Roll to form a tight, neat cylinder and wrap in the remaining clingfilm. Repeat for the other three veal escalopes. Once rolled, chill the veal wraps in the refrigerator for 30 minutes to firm them up before cooking.

4 When you're ready to cook the wraps, preheat the oven to 180°C/fan 160°C/gas mark 4. Remove the clingfilm and tie each wrap securely with string, looping the string around each wrap 3 or 4 times. Drizzle with oil and seal in a hot pan until golden brown on the outside. Transfer to a baking sheet and bake for 8–12 minutes, then remove from the oven and leave to rest for 5 minutes. Slice each roll into discs about 2cm (¾in) thick to serve.

I'd probably cook anything that has the word 'crown' in the title. Luckily, this classic British dish is fit for a queen. It looks seriously impressive and can be eaten as a main course or used as a stunning centrepiece for your buffet table. The cavity in the crown is perfect for filling with sumptuous fruit (as suggested below), some stuffing (cook this separately and add it when the roast is done), or even a medley of seasonal vegetables.

CROWN of LAMB

PREP
40 minutes,
plus chilling

COOKING
35–45 minutes

SERVES 4

2 French-trimmed racks of lamb
salt and black pepper

To serve
selection of fruit (such as kumquats, figs and cranberries)
few sprigs of rosemary

1 Preheat the oven to 200°C/fan 180°C/gas mark 6.

2 Trim away as much excess fat from the racks of lamb as possible. Then, using a sharp knife, cut through the sinew between each cutlet for 2.5cm (1in) from the thickest end. Bend each of the racks into a crescent, making sure that you have the fatty side of the ribs on the inside.

3 Using a large darning needle threaded with kitchen string, carefully sew the ends of the 2 racks together to form a crown, with the bones pointing upwards and the meaty flesh forming the base. Tie another length of kitchen string around the centre of the crown. Season the crown with salt and pepper, then chill for 20 minutes in the refrigerator to set it in shape.

4 Remove the crown from the refrigerator and wrap foil around each of the bone tips. Place on a roasting tray and roast for 35 minutes for medium rare (pierce the lamb with a sharp knife – the juices should run pink), or 45 minutes for medium. When the meat is cooked how you like it, remove it from the oven and set it aside to rest for 10 minutes. Remove the foil from the bone tips and serve on a platter decorated with fruit and rosemary sprigs.

Pie fillings should be rich, velvety and very tender. For meat fillings, this means slow cooking, whereas it's essential not to overcook fish and chicken fillings.

Beef or Venison Pie

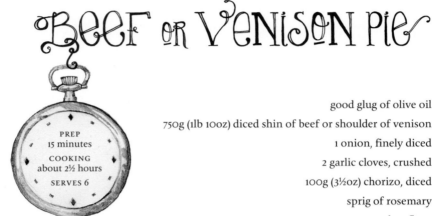

PREP
15 minutes

COOKING
about 2½ hours

SERVES 6

good glug of olive oil

750g (1lb 10oz) diced shin of beef or shoulder of venison

1 onion, finely diced

2 garlic cloves, crushed

100g (3½oz) chorizo, diced

sprig of rosemary

2 tbsp flour

500ml (18fl oz) red wine

salt and black pepper

375g (13oz) ready-rolled shortcrust pastry

1 free-range egg, beaten

1 Heat the oil in a frying pan. Blot the meat on kitchen paper, then add it to the pan and spread it out, but don't stir. After 2 minutes, stir briefly, then leave for 2 more minutes, or until it is golden brown. Remove the meat with a slotted spoon and set aside. Add the onion, garlic, chorizo and rosemary to the pan. Soften the onion, then add the meat, stirring well. Sift the flour over the mixture and stir. Cook, stirring, for 3–4 minutes.

2 Remove from the heat and add the wine a bit at a time, stirring continuously. Return to the heat, bring to the boil, reduce the heat and simmer for at least 1½ hours, adding water if it gets too dry. Season, then allow to cool.

3 Preheat the oven to 190°C/fan 170°C/gas mark 5. Cut a pastry sheet slightly larger than the circumference of a large pie dish. Reserve the offcuts. Put the filling in the dish, brush the rim with beaten egg, then place the pastry on top, squashing the extra pastry around the rim of the dish to secure. Brush with egg. Use a shape cutter to cut out shapes from the reserved pastry, arrange these on top and brush with more egg. Bake on a baking sheet in the middle of the oven for 45 minutes until the pastry is golden.

CHICKEN and ASPARAGUS PIE

PREP
15 minutes

COOKING
about 1¼ hours

SERVES 6

good glug of olive oil

500g (1lb 2oz) chicken breast, diced

1 onion, finely diced

2 garlic cloves, crushed

2 tbsp flour

200ml (7fl oz) white wine

200g (7oz) blanched asparagus tips

sprig of tarragon

100ml (3½fl oz) double cream

salt and black pepper

375g (13oz) ready-rolled shortcrust pastry

1 free-range egg, beaten

1 Heat the oil in a frying pan. Blot the chicken on some kitchen paper, add it to the pan and spread it out, but don't stir. After 2 minutes, stir briefly, then leave for 2 minutes. Remove with a slotted spoon and set aside. Add the onion and garlic. Soften the onion, then sift the flour over it and cook, stirring, for 3–4 minutes.

2 Remove from the heat. Add the wine a bit at a time, stirring continuously. Return to the heat, bring to the boil and reduce to a simmer, then add the chicken, asparagus and tarragon. After 10 minutes add the cream and season. Once everything is simmering again, turn off the heat and allow to cool.

3 To assemble and bake the pie, follow step 3 of the Beef or Venison Pie recipe, opposite.

SIMPLE FISH PIE

PREP
20 minutes

COOKING
about 1¼ hours

SERVES 6

400g (14oz) mixed filleted fish and seafood (salmon, smoked cod/haddock, prawns)

50g (1¾oz) butter

1 onion, finely diced

2 garlic cloves, crushed

2 tbsp flour

200ml (7fl oz) white wine

100ml (3½fl oz) double cream

1 tbsp capers

salt and black pepper

1 hard-boiled egg, peeled and quartered

375g (13oz) ready-rolled shortcrust pastry

1 free-range egg, beaten

1 Place the fish in a pan, barely cover with water, bring to the boil and turn off the heat and set aside. (Leave the fish in the water.) Heat the butter in a frying pan, then add the onion and garlic. Soften the onion, then sift over the flour and stir. Cook for 3–4 minutes, stirring well. Remove from the heat and add the wine a bit at a time, stirring continuously. Return to the heat, bring to the boil and reduce to a simmer.

2 Flake the fish into fairly large pieces, then add it to the mixture along with the cream and capers. Bring to a simmer, turn off the heat, season, then add the hard-boiled egg. Allow to cool.

3 To assemble and bake the pie, follow step 3 of the Beef or Venison Pie recipe, opposite.

Mum, mum... are you in there?

If you like 'The Addams Family', you'll love this. Sometimes I hide toy coffins at the bottom of the couscous! Beyond the visuals, though, it's a really healthy dish. Buy seasonal vegetables and make your own dipping sauces such as peppered houmous, aubergine or mackerel mousse, or tzatziki. Weird and fabulous!

SALAD CEMETERY

PREP
30 minutes
SERVES 4

2 tsp squid ink (available from good fishmongers) or 1 tsp black food colouring

200ml (7fl oz) just-boiled water

150g (5½oz) couscous

1 tsp olive oil

salt and black pepper

assorted micro herbs (available from large supermarkets), such as red radish, rocket, mizuna, mustard and cress, coriander and pea shoots

assorted miniature vegetables (available from large supermarkets), such as baby courgettes, radishes, young fennel, baby carrots, baby pak choi – 150g (5½oz) per type of vegetable used

selection of dips, such as houmous or tzatziki, to serve

1 Mix the ink or food colouring with the water in a measuring jug, then pour this over the couscous in a large bowl. Add the oil and season to taste with salt and pepper. Cover the bowl with clingfilm and set aside for about 10 minutes until all the liquid is absorbed and the couscous has puffed up. Fluff up the grains with a fork.

2 Transfer the coloured couscous to a serving dish and arrange the herbs and vegetables on top, poking these into the couscous as if you were planting a miniature garden.

3 Serve with a selection of dips, giving each guest a small pair of scissors to allow them to trim their own micro herbs.

Shake up your evening with these breathtaking artichoke maracas. Whenever I cook fresh artichoke hearts, I'm loath to chuck the remaining inedible leaves away. So, use them to serve this dip in and save on washing-up – problem solved! The contrast of the muted pink dip against the green flower is stunning and, as a bonus, it's also completely yummy.

BEETROOT and ARTICHOKE maracas

PREP
30 minutes
MAKES 8

150g (5½oz) cooked beetroot, roughly chopped
8 artichoke hearts from a jar, roughly chopped
250g (9oz) ricotta cheese
handful of chives, finely chopped, plus extra to garnish
1 tbsp extra-virgin olive oil
juice of ½ lemon
salt and black pepper
8 globe artichokes
Melba Toast, to serve (*see* page 72)

1 Purée the beetroot and artichoke hearts using a food processor or handheld blender. Using a wooden spoon, fold in the ricotta, chives, olive oil and lemon juice, then season to taste.

2 Cut the hearts out of the globe artichokes using a small, sharp knife, and discard these (or use in another recipe). Either spoon the dip into the centre of each artichoke (where the heart was), or fit a piping bag with a round nozzle and pipe the dip into the cavity.

3 Either stand each artichoke in its own individual glass to serve or arrange all 8 in a heavy glass or vase to make an impact at the table.

4 Serve with homemade Melba Toast to dip into the artichoke hearts.

In the early 20th century, aspic (a savoury jelly made from meat stock) was considered chic. Chefs loved to showcase their creations, and there were no boundaries as to what you could suspend in aspic. I think it's visually stunning and I understand why cooks are charmed by it. I use aspic to complement a dish, and the humble mushroom loaf is a great example of this.

MUSHROOM ASPIC Loaves

PREP
30 minutes, plus
soaking and chilling

COOKING
15 minutes

SERVES 6

30g (1oz) dried porcini mushrooms

200ml (7fl oz) warm water

50ml (2fl oz) olive oil

30g (1oz) butter

3 shallots, finely diced

1 garlic clove, finely diced

400g (14oz) mixed mushrooms, such as portobello, shiitake, oyster, enoki and brown beech

salt and black pepper

2 tbsp dry sherry

3 leaves gelatine

6 sprigs of thyme

1 Soak the dried porcini mushrooms in the warm water for around 30 minutes, until rehydrated.

2 Meanwhile, heat the olive oil and butter in a large frying pan and fry the shallots and garlic for 5 minutes over a medium heat until transparent. Add the mixed mushrooms (in batches, if necessary) and fry for 4–5 minutes. Season to taste with salt and pepper. Transfer to a plate covered with kitchen paper to drain.

3 Strain the rehydrated porcini mushrooms, retaining the soaking liquid. Transfer this to a small saucepan along with the sherry.

4 Soak the gelatine in a bowl of cold water for 4–5 minutes or following the packet instructions, allowing it to swell. Remove from the water and

gently squeeze out the excess liquid. Add the gelatine to the mushroom stock, then stir this over a medium heat until the gelatine has melted entirely. Remove from the heat.

5 Now assemble the loaves. Dip each sprig of thyme in turn into the stock, then place it on the bottom of one of 6 mini loaf tins. Slice any mushrooms that are too large to fit. Dip individual mushrooms (or mushroom slices) into the stock and layer them into the loaf tins.

6 Pour in the remaining stock to fill each tin to the top. Arrange the tins in a roasting tin and leave in the refrigerator for 2 hours. Serve with a herb salad and warm Melba Toast (*see* page 72). Run the tip of a small pointed knife around the top edge of the moulds to loosen them and serve.

HOW TO MAKE A
BOTTLED BUTTERFLY DISPLAY

The art of preserving insects and butterflies in a lifelike display was incredibly popular in the Victorian era and was an effective way for people to show off any 'trophies' from their visits to exotic countries. They especially loved to bring back taxidermy, which nowadays provokes mixed feelings, but soaring prices on internet auction houses and diminishing finds at local sales indicates that both are coming back into vogue! So here is a gentle introduction to help you get ahead of the fashion.

YOU WILL NEED

globe-shaped bowl, or any interesting glass vessel ❦ moss and twigs (these can be found in your garden or any wooded area) ❦ green floral foam ❦ china teacup ❦ small fake flowers ❦ butterflies (*see* pages 90–93) ❦ buttons, beads, rocks or anything else that takes your fancy ❦ metal or glass base to support the bowl (I have used a large candleholder here)

STEP 1 Fill the glass vessel with moss in order to create a natural-looking environment.

STEP 2 Place some twigs in the moss so that they stand up.

STEP 3 Add some floral foam to a teacup and place some flowers and a butterfly in the cup.

STEP 4 Place the teacup on top of the moss.

STEP 5 Add anything else that takes your fancy.

STEP 6 Finally, place the bowl on the plinth or candleholder and place in the centre of your dinner table.

These are a stunning addition to your evening tea-party buffet and they are simple to make. Choose the freshest fruits you can find. I like to use a variety of sizes and colours for maximum visual effect. There are many different types of sugar available, but white granulated and caster work best here, and each gives a slightly different effect. If you would like to follow a colour theme, try colouring your sugar by adding a few drops of food colouring to a jar of white sugar, shaking vigorously, then tipping it on to a tray covered with nonstick baking paper to dry overnight.

SUGARED FRUITS

PREP
30 minutes,
plus setting
SERVES 6–8

2 free-range egg whites, beaten

500g (1lb 2oz) granulated sugar

500g (1lb 2oz) caster sugar

assorted whole fruits (those with stems work best) –
we used 500g (1lb 2oz) grapes, 400g (14oz) strawberries, 4 pears and 8 apples

1 Put the egg white in one bowl, the granulated sugar in another, and the caster sugar in a third.

2 Take a piece of fruit and, holding it by the stem, dip it into the egg white, shake away the excess and then dip it into one of the sugars to coat. Place it on a tray and repeat with the remaining fruit. Leave to set for 1 hour at room temperature.

3 If there are bare patches on your fruit, or if you want a denser covering of sugar, repeat the process in step 2.

4 Arranged the sugared fruits on a cake stand and place it in the centre of your dinner table.

Charlie loved his chocolate figs.

He ate twelve dozen at every gig.

He never quite felt like a pig,

Because it's fruit... and he loved his chocolate figs!

CHARLIE'S CHOCOLATE FIGS
DIPPED IN SEA SALT

PREP
10 minutes,
plus chilling

MAKES 12

12 small, ripe figs
150g (5½oz) plain dark chocolate
sea salt flakes, for sprinkling

1 Trim the fig stems to neaten them, but don't remove them entirely (you'll need something to pick the figs up with when dipping them in the chocolate).

2 Break the chocolate into pieces and melt it in a bowl set over a saucepan of barely simmering water, making sure that the base of the bowl doesn't touch the water. Take off the heat.

3 Holding them by their stems, dip the figs, one by one, in the melted chocolate so that the chocolate comes three-quarters of the way up the side of each fruit. Place on a baking sheet covered with nonstick baking paper.

4 While the chocolate is still wet, sprinkle each fig with sea salt flakes, then set them aside in a cool place for 30 minutes to harden.

Pear and caramel is a winning combination and crunchy shortcrust pastry turns it into a sublime pudding, perfect for any tea party. I like to add a dollop of good vanilla ice cream for contrast. Choose a pear with a lovely tall shape (like a Conference) for maximum visual impact.

PEAR DUMPLINGS
WITH A CARAMEL GLAZE

350g (12oz) plain flour

2 tsp baking powder

1 tsp salt

225g (8oz) vegetable shortening

225ml (8fl oz) milk

6 ripe pears, peeled but with the stalks left on

40g (1½oz) brown sugar

1 tsp ground cinnamon

70g (2½oz) macadamia nuts, roughly chopped

15g (½oz) butter, plus extra to dot on the pears

PREP
30 minutes

COOKING
45–55 minutes

SERVES 6

For the caramel glaze

100g (3½oz) dark brown sugar

2 tbsp water

10g (¼oz) butter

1 Preheat the oven to 190°C/fan 170°C/gas mark 5 and lightly grease a baking sheet.

2 Combine the flour, baking powder and salt in a bowl, then rub in the vegetable shortening until the mixture resembles breadcrumbs. Gradually add the milk, stirring to produce a soft dough. Turn the dough out on to a lightly floured surface, then roll it into a 40cm (16in) square. Using a knife, cut the rectangle into 6 even-sized squares.

3 Core each pear from the bottom, leaving the top 5cm (2in) of the pear and the stalk intact.

4 Mix together the sugar, cinnamon, nuts and butter. Press 2 tsp of the mixture firmly into the centre of each pear, and place each on a pastry square. Dot the pears with a little more butter. Moisten the inside edges of each of the pastry squares with water, then bring the 4 corners up around the pear, pinching to seal (the top of each pear should be poking out). Stand the pears on the prepared baking sheet and bake for 40–50 minutes, covering with foil after 30 minutes.

5 To make the glaze, heat the sugar and water in a saucepan over a low heat. Once the sugar has melted, increase the heat and allow the glaze to reduce for about 3 minutes. Remove from the heat, add the butter and stir until it has melted. Drizzle each pear with some glaze before serving.

French chef Marie-Antoine Carême named the Charlotte Russe in honour of his Russian employer in the early 19th century. Whenever I make this dessert, I can't help feeling jealous that no one has named a dessert after me yet! The basic ingredients are sponge fingers, cream and fruit, but once you've mastered the basics you can be as experimental as you like. This is my favoured version for taste and colour sensations.

STRAWBERRY AND RASPBERRY CHARLOTTE RUSSE

PREP
20 minutes,
plus soaking
and chilling

SERVES 6

6 gelatine leaves
750g (1lb 10oz) strawberries, hulled
250g (9oz) raspberries
60g (2¼oz) caster sugar
75ml (2½fl oz) single cream
250g (9oz) sponge fingers

1 Soak the gelatine leaves in a bowl of water for 10 minutes. Drain the gelatine leaves, squeeze out the excess water and set aside.

2 Reserve some fruits to decorate the cake and blend the remainder in a food processor. Pass the purée through a sieve and discard the raspberry seeds. In a saucepan, mix a quarter of the fruit purée with the sugar over a medium heat until the sugar has dissolved. Add the gelatine leaves and stir. Stir in the remaining fruit purée and, finally, the cream. Don't allow it to boil. Once the gelatine has dissolved, remove the fruit cream from the heat.

3 Line the base of a charlotte mould (or cake tin or soufflé dish) with sponge fingers then stand some more upright around the edge. Pour the fruit cream into the centre. Arrange the remaining biscuits on top of the cream.

4 Cover the cake with clingfilm and refrigerate for 4 hours. To serve, run the bottom of the mould under a warm tap for a few seconds then invert the cake on to a clean plate. Top the cake with the reserved fruits and serve cold.

HEALTH WARNING: this is a seriously rich pudding – make sure you have run around the house several times before you enjoy the buttery, sugary, spicy gingerbread loveliness. The pudding is delicious by itself, but adding brandy to the eggnog cream really turns this dish into something for the grown-ups.

Gingerbread Pudding
with Eggnog Cream

PREP 15–20 minutes
COOKING 40–55 minutes
SERVES 6

115g (4oz) butter, softened, plus extra for greasing

generous 250g (9oz) plain flour

1½ tsp bicarbonate of soda

1½ tsp ground ginger

1 tsp ground cinnamon

½ tsp salt

½ tsp ground allspice

½ tsp ground nutmeg

115g (4oz) soft brown sugar

1 free-range egg

325g (11½oz) molasses

250ml (9fl oz) water

55g (2oz) muscovado sugar

For the topping

350ml (12fl oz) hot water

115g (4oz) melted butter

For the eggnog cream

150ml (5fl oz) double cream

generous glug of brandy (optional)

50ml (2fl oz) eggnog (available in all good supermarkets)

1 Preheat the oven to 170°C/fan 150°C/between gas marks 3 and 4. Grease a 33 × 23cm (13 × 9in) baking tin and line with nonstick baking paper.

2 Sieve the flour, bicarbonate of soda, ginger, cinnamon, salt, allspice and nutmeg together in a medium-sized bowl and set aside.

3 In a large bowl, beat the softened butter together with the soft brown sugar using an electric whisk on a medium speed until creamy. Add the egg and beat until well combined. Reduce the mixer speed to low. Beat in a little of the flour mixture, then a little of the molasses, then a little of the water. Continue in this way until all the ingredients are blended. Pour the mixture into the prepared baking tin and sprinkle with the muscovado sugar. Set aside.

4 For the topping, combine the hot water and butter in a medium-sized bowl, then pour over the cake mixture. Bake for 40–55 minutes or until the gingerbread is cracked on top and a toothpick inserted into the centre comes out clean.

5 Meanwhile, prepare the eggnog cream. Whip the double cream until it forms soft peaks. If you like a little kick, add some brandy to your eggnog at this stage, then fold it into the cream. Serve the warm pudding with the eggnog cream.

This classic French cake is made from profiteroles held together by caramel to form a conical tower. It was traditionally served at celebrations and was often decorated with spun sugar and sugared nuts – croquembouche means 'crunch in the mouth'.

WHITE AND DARK CHOCOLATE CROQUEMBOUCHE

PREP
2 hours

COOKING
35 minutes

SERVES 60

For the pastry

140g (5oz) butter

250ml (9fl oz) water

150g (5½oz) plain flour, sieved

4 free-range eggs, beaten

For the chocolate cream

1.2 litres (2 pints) double cream

150g (5½oz) icing sugar

20g (¾oz) dark cocoa powder

20g (¾oz) white cocoa powder

For the caramel sauce

450g (1lb) caster sugar

600ml (1 pint) water

1 Preheat the oven to 220°C/fan 200°C/gas mark 7 and line 2 baking sheets with baking paper.

2 For the pastry, melt the butter in the water in a saucepan over a medium heat and bring to the boil. Add all the flour and stir continuously with a wooden spoon. Cook for 2 minutes until the mixture pulls away from the pan, forming a ball, then remove from the heat. Transfer to a large bowl and stir for 1 more minute to cool the dough. Add the egg a little at a time, mixing the dough until smooth after each addition, until fully incorporated. Fit a piping bag with a star-shaped nozzle and spoon the dough into the bag. Pipe 2.5cm (1in) balls of dough on to the baking sheets. Bake in batches for 25 minutes until the pastry balls have risen and are golden.

3 To make the filling, put the cream and icing sugar in a large bowl and whisk until it forms soft peaks. Separate into 2 equal portions and, using a wooden spoon, fold the dark cocoa powder into one and the white into the other.

4 Pierce a hole in the base of each bun. Fit two clean piping bags with clean nozzles. Pipe white chocolate cream into half the buns and dark chocolate cream into the other half. Set aside.

5 To make the caramel, put the sugar and half the water in a heavy-based saucepan over a medium heat. Don't allow the water to boil and don't stir the caramel. Once the sugar has dissolved, increase the heat and boil the mixture until it becomes caramel in colour. Tip in the remaining water. Stir until you have a smooth sauce, then remove from the heat and set aside to cool.

6 To assemble, place a cardboard cone in the centre of a large plate. One by one, dip each bun into the caramel sauce and set it in place, forming a round of buns around the base of the cone. Follow with another round on top. Keep building in this way, using the caramel to cement the buns together, until you have formed a tall cone. Drizzle with the remaining caramel sauce and embellish with decorations of your choice.

I find the seductive smell of coconut baking in the oven reason alone to make these squidgy macaroons. They are a dainty, elegant nibble, perfect for any tea-party table. As the primary flavours are chocolate and coconut, make sure you choose the best – your chocolate should be dark and at least 70 per cent cocoa solids, and your coconut should be freshly shredded. If you can't find this, the packaged type will suffice.

CHOCOLATE COCONUT MACAROONS

PREP
25 minutes,
plus setting
COOKING
15–18 minutes
MAKES 24

1 free-range egg white
200g (7oz) caster sugar
30g (1oz) plain flour
20g (¾oz) cocoa powder
200g (7oz) fresh coconut, coarsely grated
100g (3½oz) dark chocolate, broken into pieces
100g (3½oz) white chocolate, broken into pieces

1 Preheat the oven to 180°C/fan 160°C/gas mark 4 and line 2 baking sheets with nonstick baking paper. In a clean bowl, whisk the egg white until stiff, then gradually add the sugar, whisking continuously until thick and glossy. Sift the flour, then fold into the egg white mixture along with the cocoa powder and coconut until completely combined.

2 Using an 8cm (3¼in) shape cutter as a mould, fill with tablespoonfuls of the mixture on the prepared baking sheets (12 on each). Bake for 15–18 minutes until golden around the edges and just starting to brown on top. Leave to cool a little, then transfer to a wire rack to cool completely.

3 Melt the dark chocolate in a bowl set over a saucepan of barely simmering water, ensuring the base of the bowl doesn't touch the water. Remove the chocolate from the heat, allow it to cool slightly, then transfer to a disposable piping bag. Cut a tiny hole at the bag's point and decorate half the macaroons by piping lines of chocolate back and forth across the top. Repeat for the other half of the macaroons, using a new piping bag and the white chocolate. Allow the chocolate to set for 20 minutes. The macaroons will keep in an airtight container for 2 days.

This pudding is so quick to make that sometimes I feel I should apologize to my guests for spending so little time on it. It tastes wonderful, too, especially with the addition of the spiced walnuts (you will have leftovers from the recipe, but it's no hardship as they make very moreish nibbles). I really like the contrast between the crunch and spiciness of the walnuts and the creamy texture of the posset. I hope you do, too.

ORANGE POSSETS WITH SPICED WALNUTS

For the orange possets

2 × 284ml cartons double cream

100g (3½oz) caster sugar

100ml (3½fl oz) orange juice

50ml (2fl oz) lemon juice

2 tbsp orange liqueur (optional)

For the spiced walnuts

1 tbsp honey

2 tsp olive oil

1 tbsp water

200g (7oz) walnut halves

½ tsp coarse salt

2 tbsp sugar

1 tsp ground cumin

½ tsp ground allspice

½ tsp ground cinnamon

⅛ tsp cayenne pepper

PREP
25 minutes,
plus chilling
COOKING
10 minutes
SERVES 4

1 To make the possets, gently heat the cream and sugar in a small pan. Stir constantly until the sugar has dissolved, then heat until almost boiling. Cook gently for about 3 minutes, stirring all the time – be careful not to let it boil over.

2 Remove from the heat and stir in the fruit juices, then add the liqueur, if using. Leave to cool for 5 minutes (this is especially important if you're using delicate glasses to serve). Pour into serving dishes and chill in the refrigerator for at least 4 hours, until ready to use.

3 For the spiced walnuts, line a large baking sheet with foil. Heat the honey, olive oil and water in a large nonstick frying pan over a medium heat, until fully combined. Add the walnuts and toss to coat thoroughly.

4 Sprinkle the salt, sugar, cumin, allspice, cinnamon and cayenne pepper over the nuts and stir until fully coated. Continue to cook over a medium heat for 4–5 minutes, stirring continuously, until the nuts are slightly browned.

5 Transfer the nuts to the prepared baking sheet and spread to form a single layer. Allow to cool completely before using. Place 2 or 3 walnuts on top of each posset. Store the remaining spiced walnuts in an airtight container.

Why is this choc-ice so posh? Because the sorbet is made from a very lovely bottle of red wine, and is served in an edible dark-chocolate saucer (so no washing-up afterwards!). The blackberries intensify the fruitiness of the wine, and also lend a beautiful grape colour. Once you've mastered the art of making chocolate saucers, there are plenty of ways to use them for both adults' and childrens' parties – let your imagination run riot!

A VERY POSH CHOC-ICE

PREP
40 minutes,
plus churning,
freezing
and chilling
SERVES 6

1 free-range egg white

225g (8oz) blackberries

225ml (8fl oz) water

115g (4oz) caster sugar

175ml (6fl oz) Cabernet Sauvignon or other robust red wine

2 tsp lemon juice

fresh kumquats, to decorate

For the chocolate saucers

150g (5½oz) dark chocolate

6 regular-sized balloons

1 Whisk the egg white using an electric whisk until stiff peaks form. Set aside.

2 Blend the blackberries, water, caster sugar, wine and lemon juice with a handheld blender until smooth. Transfer to a bowl and stir in the whisked egg white. Cover with clingfilm and chill in the refrigerator for about 30 minutes.

3 Pour the mixture into an ice-cream maker with the paddle running. Freeze until the desired consistency is achieved (it should be firm and scoopable) then transfer to the freezer.

4 To make the chocolate saucers, break the chocolate into pieces and melt it in a bowl set over a saucepan of barely simmering water, making sure that the base of the bowl doesn't touch the water. Blow up the balloons, filling

them about a quarter full. Once you've tied the balloons closed, wash them carefully and allow them to air-dry.

5 Line a baking sheet with nonstick baking paper. Holding the balloons by their ends, dip them one by one into the melted chocolate until the chocolate comes about halfway up the sides. Set the dipped balloons on the prepared baking sheet. Refrigerate for 10–15 minutes until the chocolate has set.

6 Using a needle, gently poke a small hole at the knotted end of each balloon, to let the air seep out slowly so the balloon does not explode and break the saucer. Remove the balloons, scoop sorbet into the saucers and serve immediately, decorated with kumquats.

This rich, sensuous sorbet is a must for chocoholics. There's no dairy in this recipe, which means you can really enjoy the pure, unadulterated taste of chocolate. It's luxurious in taste, and could even be classified as good for you; dark chocolate is rich in flavonoids and is known to help release endorphins (happy hormones). Now fetch me a spoon!

DARK CHOCOLATE SORBET

PREP
20 minutes, plus chilling, churning and freezing
SERVES 4–6

500ml (18fl oz) water

200g (7oz) caster sugar

200g (7oz) dark chocolate (at least 70 per cent cocoa solids), chopped into small pieces

pinch of salt

2 tbsp coffee liqueur (optional)

1 Pour the water into a large saucepan and heat on the stove over a high heat. Add the sugar and stir. Bring the mixture to a boil and stir until all the sugar is dissolved. Add the chocolate pieces, then turn off the heat and mix vigorously until the chocolate has melted. You should be left with a mouth-watering, silky smooth looking mixture (avoid the temptation to dive into it!). Add the salt and coffee liqueur and stir again to incorporate. Allow to cool.

2 Chill the chocolate mixture in the refrigerator for 2 hours, then churn it in an ice-cream maker until the desired consistency is achieved (the sorbet should be firm and scoopable) then transfer to the freezer. If you don't have an ice-cream maker, partially freeze the sorbet in a shallow container with a lid (or you can cover the container with clingfilm) for 1 hour, then remove and blend briefly in a food processor. Return it to the freezer and blend again after 1 hour. Repeat the process again (the more you do it, the smaller the ice crystals become), then allow to set completely. The mixture won't be as smooth as one from an ice-cream maker, but the taste is still sensational.

3 The sorbet will freeze into quite a hard consistency, so remove it from the freezer 5–10 minutes before serving.

A granita is a frozen ice dessert, much like a sorbet but with larger ice crystals. Granitas are easy to make and you can choose whatever flavours you desire. I like this lemon-lime combination because sometimes, after a particularly rich meal, all you want is something sharp, sweet, clean and light. I have been known to add some finely chopped basil or mint leaves to the mix. Not only do they enhance the flavour, but the tiny green flecks look fantastic among the snowy white clouds of ice.

LEMON-LIME GRANITA

PREP
20 minutes,
plus chilling
and freezing

COOKING
10 minutes

SERVES 4

200g (7oz) caster sugar

275ml (9½fl oz) cold water

juice of 4 lemons and rind of 2

juice of 5 limes and rind of 2

handful of basil or mint, finely chopped (optional)

1 Place the sugar, water and lemon and lime rind in a large saucepan and slowly bring to a simmering boil over a gentle heat. Stir until the sugar is dissolved, then remove from the heat and cool slightly.

2 Pour the lemon and lime juices into the sugary syrup and strain. Add the mint or basil, if using, and stir to evenly distribute the herbs, then tip the mixture into a shallow container with a lid (or you can cover the container with clingfilm) and place in a freezer.

3 After 1 hour, remove the container and break up the contents with a fork. You don't need to mash it up too much as a granita is meant to have quite a grainy texture. Return to the freezer and repeat the process twice. You should now have a mass of snowy crystals. It can remain in the freezer for 3–4 hours – any longer and it will turn quite hard, but don't worry because about half an hour before serving time you can place the granita in the refrigerator, then fork it up again when it's a little softer.

In western folklore, Bloody Mary was a witch. It was believed that if you stood in front of a mirror and said her name three times she would appear in the mirror. We can thank her for numerous films, computer games, TV programmes and the infamous drink. So let's raise our glasses to Mary: 'Thank you Bloody Mary, thank you Bloody Mary, thank you Bloody Mary!'

BLOODY MARY SHOTS

PREP
20 minutes
SERVES 6

½ shallot, roughly chopped

1 tbsp freshly grated horseradish

1½ sticks of celery, roughly chopped

200g (7oz) chopped tomatoes

¼ tsp celery salt, plus an extra 2 tbsp to decorate the glasses

1½ tbsp Worcestershire sauce

½–1 tsp Tabasco sauce

¼ tsp black pepper

juice of ½ lemon (reserve the unjuiced half for wetting the glass rims)

500ml (18fl oz) tomato juice

4 tbsp vodka

1 tbsp Amontillado or other dry sherry

1 Place the shallot, horseradish, 1 stick of celery, tomatoes, celery salt, Worcestershire sauce, Tabasco, black pepper and lemon juice in a liquidizer and blend until smooth. Strain the mixture through a sieve, using the back of a metal spoon to push it through. Stir in the tomato juice, vodka and sherry.

2 Just before serving, wet the rim of 6 small glasses with the reserved lemon half, then turn each one upside-down and dip it in a saucer of celery salt, to coat the rim. Divide the Bloody Mary between the glasses. Trim the remaining half-stick of celery, cut it in half lengthways, then cut each length into 3 batons of equal size, using a slanted cut. Place a celery baton in each glass to serve.

Rosie Lee. This is probably the most famous and well-used example of Cockney rhyming slang, and it means 'tea'. 'Ooohh... I'd love a cup of Rosie, please, gran!' (My gran is an East Londoner with the family name of Lee.) For the non-alcoholic version of this drink, swap the vodka and bubbly for tonic water. Both versions of this drink are steeped in decadence and visually stunning.

Rosie Lee Loves Her Tea

PREP
5 minutes,
plus steeping
and chilling

SERVES 6

6 tbsp loose rosebud tea

300ml (½ pint) just-boiled water

100g (3½oz) caster sugar, or to taste

100ml (3½fl oz) vodka, chilled

1 bottle of Champagne or sparkling white wine, chilled

ice cubes

edible rose petals, to decorate

1 Share the rosebud tea between 2 paper tea filter bags and steep these in the water in a measuring jug for 8 minutes, adding the sugar and stirring until dissolved. Remove the tea bags. (Alternatively, put the tea loose into the water and strain after steeping.) Chill the tea in the refrigerator for 30 minutes.

2 Add the vodka and bubbly (or 850ml/1½ pints tonic water), stir to mix, then pour into 6 teacups. Add ice cubes.

3 Decorate with an edible rose petal or two, then serve immediately.

We British have welcomed green tea with open arms. At every event I hold it's a staple, with one in four people asking for it. That's pretty impressive. It's lighter and earthier than black tea and, apparently, it's very good for you. If you drink four cups a day, you will be healthier and live longer. Perhaps you'll be richer, too. With this in mind, you can be guilt-free when you try my delicious, grassy Green Tea and Pear Cocktail.

GREEN TEA AND PEAR COCKTAIL

PREP
5 minutes,
plus steeping
and chilling

SERVES 6

12 green tea bags

300ml (½ pint) just-boiled water

100g (3½oz) caster sugar, or to taste

100ml (3½fl oz) vodka

850ml (1½ pints) pear juice (or a pear, apple and grape juice mixture)

ice cubes

lime rind, to garnish

1 Steep the tea bags in the water in a measuring jug for 3 minutes, adding the sugar and stirring until dissolved. Remove the tea bags. Chill the tea in the refrigerator for 30 minutes.

2 Add the vodka and fruit juice, stir to mix, then pour into 6 teacups. Add ice cubes.

3 Garnish with lime rind, then serve immediately.

This chic Champagne cocktail transports me to 'The Little Shop of Horrors'. I like to think that if I let one of the wild hibiscus flowers grow it might turn into Audrey II, which would certainly make for an interesting party. Wild hibiscus buds in syrup are easy to get hold of on the internet and keep for a very long time. The flowers and their syrup add a delicious, fruity taste and the blooms are very juicy, like big cherries filled with sweet bubbles.

WILD HIBISCUS CHAMPAGNE

PREP
1 minute

SERVES 6

6 wild hibiscus flowers in syrup

1 bottle of Champagne or sparkling white wine, chilled

1 Place a hibiscus flower and 1 teaspoon of the syrup in the bottom of each glass and, when the party starts, add the chilled bubbly.

2 Serve immediately and watch people smile with delight as you take credit for creating such a fancy drink!

In the past, I have been accused of creating drinks that are a touch on the feminine side. Of course, I disagree totally, as many male party-goers love a Lavender Pearl cocktail! But I must listen to my customers and, when I'm asked for a 'man's drink' nowadays, I offer them Gunfire. This is the kind of thing a big, strong pirate would have drunk on a cold night, so off I go to walk the plank and put the kettle on.

PREP
5 minutes,
plus steeping
and chilling

SERVES 6

6 English Breakfast tea bags

300ml (½ pint) just-boiled water

85g (3oz) caster sugar,
or to taste

100ml (3½fl oz) dark rum

orange rind, to decorate

1 Steep the tea bags in the water in a measuring jug for 4 minutes, adding the sugar and stirring until dissolved. Remove the tea bags. Chill the tea in the refrigerator for 30 minutes.

2 Add the rum, stir to mix, then pour into 6 teacups.

3 Decorate with orange rind, then serve immediately.

While hosting a children's tea party on a very hot day, for refreshment I made some iced green-jasmine tea from the contents of my tea basket, adding berries for colour. It was an instant hit – I simply could not make it quickly enough for the children. Later, during the party, the adults cracked open a bottle of Champagne, which we added to our chilled tea – and our signature cocktail was born.

GREEN-JASMINE TEA BUBBLES

PREP
5 minutes,
plus steeping
and cooling

SERVES
5 without alcohol
and 10 with

5 green-jasmine tea bags or 5 tbsp loose green-jasmine tea

200ml (7fl oz) just-boiled water

3 tbsp caster sugar, or to taste

500ml (18fl oz) cold water

handful of raspberries and blackberries (optional)

1 bottle of good Champagne, chilled (optional)

1 Steep the tea bags or loose tea in a measuring jug in the just-boiled water for 1 minute, adding the sugar and stirring until dissolved. Remove the tea bags, or strain to remove the loose tea, then add the cold water.

2 Taste the tea for strength, adding a touch more cold water if it's too strong, then put it in the refrigerator to chill further for 30 minutes. (If you can't wait, add a few ice cubes to speed up the chilling process.)

3 Serve in vintage teacups. For a bit of extra colour, put a couple of berries into each cup before pouring, if liked. For the alcoholic version, simply half-fill the cup with tea, then top up with an equal measure of bubbly.

OUR FAMOUS RECIPE FOR

Teana Colada

PREP
10 minutes,
plus steeping
and chilling

SERVES 4

12 black tea bags
300ml (½ pint) just-boiled water
50g (1¾oz) caster sugar
400ml can coconut milk
100ml (3½fl oz) dark rum
ice cubes

1 Steep the tea bags in the water in a measuring jug for 4 minutes, adding the sugar and stirring until dissolved. Remove the tea bags. Chill the tea in the refrigerator for 30 minutes.

2 Empty the coconut milk into a jug and stir it well. Pour the cooled tea syrup and rum into a cocktail shaker with ice and shake until your bits wobble – about 5–10 seconds. Add this to the coconut milk and blitz briefly with a handheld mixer to blend.

3 Pour the cocktail into 4 glasses. Add ice cubes.

4 Decorate with cocktail umbrellas and vintage cocktail stirrers, then serve immediately.

The original G and T, or gin and tonic, was developed by an army of the East India Company. In India, in the 18th century, tonic water was frequently consumed because it contained high levels of the antimalarial substance quinine. Gin did a grand job of hiding the bitter taste of the quinine. Nowadays, this cocktail is incredibly popular, but the quinine levels in tonic water are much lower. Here is my take on the classic. I like to keep the drink light and fresh to pay tribute to the juniper berry. If G and T is really not your tipple, though, why not try a V and T? Vodka also works very well with Earl Grey and lemon.

SAFFRON G AND TEA SHOTS

PREP
5 minutes,
plus chilling
SERVES 8

6 Earl Grey tea bags
200ml (7fl oz) just-boiled water
50g (1¾oz) caster sugar, or to taste
200ml (7fl oz) gin
juice of 1½ lemons
crushed ice
a few pinches of saffron, to decorate (optional)

1 Steep the tea bags in the water in a measuring jug for 4 minutes, adding the sugar and stirring until dissolved. Remove the tea bags.

2 Fill up to 500ml (18fl oz) with cold water and refrigerate for 1 hour, or longer if you have time.

3 Remove from the refrigerator and add the gin, lemon juice and ice.

4 Serve either in teacups or tiny glasses. For a real treat, add a pinch of saffron to each shot.

The perfect pearl is round, smooth and iridescent. These gorgeous gemstones are valued most highly when they originate from the sea rather than from freshwater sources. My Lavender Pearl cocktail complements this perfectly. Use the best-quality ingredients you can afford and watch the lavender tones shine in the moonlight as you indulge in sense, vision and taste.

LAVENDER PEARL

PREP
10 minutes,
plus steeping
and chilling
SERVES 4

2 tbsp loose white tea

1 tbsp lavender petals

150ml (5fl oz) just-boiled water

70g (2½oz) caster sugar, or to taste

100ml (3½fl oz) vodka

ice cubes

100ml (3½fl oz) Prosecco, chilled

1 Place the tea and lavender petals in a paper tea filter bag and steep in the just-boiled water in a measuring jug for 4 minutes, adding the sugar and stirring until dissolved. Remove the tea bags. (Alternatively, put the tea and lavender loose into the water and strain after steeping.) Chill the tea in the refrigerator for 30 minutes.

2 Pour the cooled tea syrup and vodka into a cocktail shaker with ice and shake for 5–10 seconds.

3 Strain into 4 glasses and top with the Prosecco.

PARLOUR GAMES

Playing games encourages laughter and closeness and helps push day-to-day thoughts and worries to one side as the players become engulfed in the moment. Parlour games are a wonderful form of escapism, and are perfect for a tea party. Below are a few of my favourites.

Guess the clothing era

Ask everyone to wear a piece of vintage clothing to your party. Each person must do a bit of research to ascertain the correct era or year of their clothing beforehand – for example, they might plump for a 1960s waistcoat. The rest of the guests then try to guess the vintage of the piece of clothing.

Guess the musical era

You'll need two teams and around five songs for each team. You'll need to know the year of release for each one. Practise the songs and some dance moves to showcase them. The other team get a point for naming the song, a point for the era and a bonus point for the actual year.

Unconventional poker

Each player is dealt one card, face down. Without peeking at it, they display the card to all the other players by licking it and sticking it to their forehead, facing outwards. This is followed by a round of betting. Players attempt to guess if they have the highest card based on the distribution of visible cards and how the other players are betting. Betting continues until players fold as they think they have a lower card than the other players. When there are only two people remaining, the winner is the person with the highest card.

Charades

Players split into two teams. A member of one team mimes the title of a film, play, book, song or musical, provided by the other team in secret, to the other members of their own team, who try to guess the title from the clues provided. There is a time limit and a number of standard gestures. Many different versions of the rules exist, so always try to agree them before you start.

Are you there, Moriarty?

Two players at a time participate in a duel. Each player is blindfolded and given something that is unlikely to hurt as a weapon, such as a rolled-up newspaper. The players start off either lying on their fronts, head to head, with a metre or so between them, or holding one another's hand in a handshake. One player asks 'Are you there, Moriarty?'. The other answers 'Yes', and the duel begins. The aim of the game is to avoid being hit by the other player. The first player to get hit is out and, when this happens, another player steps in and the game continues.

The list game

This is a memory game. The first player says 'I went to the shop and bought…' an item beginning with the letter A. The next player repeats this, then adds an item beginning with B, and so on. Test your memory skills after a few gin cocktails!

My love affair with Martin(i) began in Chicago 12 years ago. Our eyes met across a crowded bar, perched high up above the city skyline. The views were extraordinary and he stole my heart, although I couldn't help but think he was a little bitter back then. But first impressions can be deceptive... Memories come flooding back when I think of the Martini cocktail, a marvellous American invention for which we must be eternally grateful. This cocktail has a personality! When I was younger, I struggled to enjoy them, but nowadays I thoroughly appreciate their bitter undertones, and enjoy experimenting with these 'Tea Tinis'.

Basic Tea Tini

PREP
10 minutes,
plus steeping
and chilling
SERVES 4

5 tea bags of your choice

150ml (5fl oz) just-boiled water

70g (2½oz) caster sugar, or to taste

100ml (3½fl oz) vodka

30ml (1fl oz) vermouth

juice of 1 lemon

ice cubes

4 lemon wheels, to decorate

Variations

For a Flower Martini, follow the Basic Tea Tini recipe but use Lady Grey tea bags, just 50g (1¾oz) caster sugar, 50ml (2fl oz) dry vermouth, and add 30ml (1fl oz) elderflower liqueur. Decorate with mint sprigs.

For a Strawberry Martini, follow the Basic Tea Tini recipe but use strawberry fruit tea and decorate with strawberry halves.

1 Steep the tea bags in the water in a measuring jug for 4 minutes, adding the sugar and stirring until dissolved. Remove the tea bags. Chill the tea in the refrigerator for 30 minutes.

2 Mix the vodka, vermouth and lemon juice together in a measuring jug.

3 Add the tea syrup and shake in a cocktail shaker with ice for 5–10 seconds.

4 Serve chilled in glasses decorated with lemon wheels on hatpins.

WARNING: this is a seriously stunning 1980s-era cocktail. You must serve it in a transparent glass rather than a teacup, or you'll miss the spectacular sunrise.

TEA-QUILA SUNRISE

PREP
5 minutes,
plus steeping
and cooling
SERVES 4

6 Earl Grey blue flower, or Earl Grey orange blossom tea bags
100ml (3½fl oz) just-boiled water
ice cubes
100ml (3½fl oz) tequila
300ml (½ pint) orange juice
50ml (2fl oz) grenadine

1 Steep the tea bags in the water in a measuring jug for 4 minutes, then remove the tea bags. Chill the tea in the refrigerator for 30 minutes.

2 Put 2 ice cubes in the bottom of each of 4 glasses and divide the tequila between the glasses. Add the orange juice to the tea and mix together, then pour this over the top of the tequila.

3 Divide the grenadine between the 4 glasses, pouring it carefully on to the back of a teaspoon so that it sinks down the centre of the glass to the bottom, then rises up slowly through the drink. Serve immediately.

The Mojito is a very special drink to me, not just because I adore the flavours of fresh mint, rum and lime, but also because it's the favourite drink of an incredibly dear friend of mine. We have travelled around the world trying Mojitos in as many bars as we can find and laughed and cried at the various versions we have received. I dedicate this drink to Jim. This man flew across the Atlantic to help create the Oolong Mo-tea-to-go. Now that's dedication for you!

OOLONG MO-TEA-TO-GO

PREP
10 minutes, plus steeping and chilling
SERVES 4

3 tbsp loose oolong tea

250ml (9fl oz) just-boiled water

100g (3½oz) caster sugar, or to taste

8–10 sprigs of mint, plus extra to decorate

crushed ice

juice of 4 limes

100ml (3½fl oz) white rum

100ml (3½fl oz) Prosecco, chilled

1 Place the tea in a paper tea filter bag and steep this in the water in a measuring jug for 4 minutes, adding the sugar and stirring until dissolved. Remove the tea bags. (Alternatively, put the tea loose into the water and strain after steeping.) Chill for 30 minutes in the refrigerator.

2 Put the mint in a cocktail shaker with crushed ice and shake for 5–10 seconds – or until your bits wobble – to mix.

3 Add the lime juice, rum and tea syrup to the cocktail shaker. Shake for 5–10 seconds to mix and pour into 4 glasses.

4 Top each one with Prosecco and give it a quick stir. Serve decorated with mint sprigs.

STYLE

THE SCIENCE OF STYLE

Style comes from within. It's an extension of your personality. How you dress sends out signals about who you are... and who you wish to be. When you first meet someone, they may judge you by your appearance. Are first impressions accurate? Sometimes. But often not. And I'm as guilty of jumping to the wrong conclusion about someone as the next person.

Your clothes will speak a thousand words before you speak one, and if you care about the impression you make you will care for your style. I live by one golden rule: feel comfortable and confident. Simple. But it's easier said than done.

During my 'Angel-A Vintage Experience' days (*see* page 8), one of the attractions for customers would be my styling service. I'd pick a selection of outfits for every customer, and it would make my evening when I saw a face illuminated by a surprising new look. I always followed my eye and instinct, and never enquired about dress size or any details other than whether there was a certain occasion in mind.

After some years, I was hungry to learn the science of dressing. So I took a few months out and attended Image Consultancy School where I learned about body shape, weight and texture, fabric patterns, seasonal fashions, and so on. Was I any better at my job? No, but it was fun.

Let me instruct you in the science of dressing, then you can use your new-found knowledge to find your perfect vintage dress. It's important when shopping, especially for vintage clothes, to go by eye rather than by measurements; I have at

It takes time, thought and continued upkeep to ensure that your wardrobe works well for you. Most people use 10 per cent of their wardrobe 90 per cent of the time. With this in mind, your current wardrobe is a good starting point if you decide you want a makeover.

I have a rule with every item of clothing I own. I must *love* it and want to scream how much I love it! Past experience has shown that whenever I've purchased an item that *nearly* fits, or *might* work with 'that' pair of shoes, it always gets demoted to the 90 per cent part of my wardrobe.

A few pointers to get you started

1 Get yourself a scrapbook and keep pictures of anything that takes your fancy. You may not have put thought into your look, or what you like, but this is a great way to start seeing a style pattern emerging. Once you have a style (for example, mine is 1940s and fun), it's easier to dress this up or down, depending on the occasion.

2 Go through your wardrobe and try everything on. Throw away any items that are worn and old. Items that you have not worn in six months should be sold, given to charity or archived. Be strict.

3 The items that are left should be items you *love*. Lay them out and write a list of types of clothing, colours and so on. This is the easiest way to identify any gaps. I divide my items into four: top, bottom, all-in-one (dresses) and jackets.

4 Write a shopping list and decide on your budget. Never go shopping without a budget or without knowing what you want, or you could be in danger of adding to

The right foundation

It's vital to the success of this project that you have a good base. If your underwear fits poorly, you have no chance of getting the rest right. Not only will the right underwear transform a look, but caring about it makes you feel good. Having a clearout of your underwear drawer is also incredibly good for the soul!

A little science

We have all heard that black is slimming. This is because we tend to scan people visually from top to bottom and one colour allows for the flow of sight to be unbroken. The same can be said for any block colour, and small patterns have the same impact. Anywhere you add a horizontal line (belt, shoe strap, pattern on jacket, pocket) will have attention drawn to it by attracting the eye there. So only add these to places that you want to highlight.

Proportion is the next thing to consider. Take a moment to think about what you are trying to achieve. If you have a small waist, you may want to accentuate this by

wearing nipped-in dresses. If you want to look as if you have longer legs, then you may want to wear a high-waisted bottom half to create the illusion of length.

Add shoulder pads or a puff sleeve if you need some broadness on top. For any woman trying to look her best, be aware that exposing the neck and chest elegantly will help to make you look slimmer. Do this and you can't go wrong.

I told you this was scientific!

Never forget your final wardrobe. Items should all work together, and having less of the right stuff will allow your wardrobe to breathe and grow.

Happy shopping, and if you fancy adding some vintage pieces to your collection, the next page is definitely for you.

HOW TO PICK THE
PERFECT VINTAGE DRESS

Vintage clothes have already lived. They have attended glamorous balls, fabulous lunches and secret sensual cocktails with an admirer. Upon buying them, it is your responsibility to wear them to their full potential; don't over- or underdress them. Take them out to places where they will be appreciated, and you will become the woman that turns heads as she glides into a room. Picking the perfect vintage dress is an art – it takes dedication, style and a degree of elegance.

First, you have to be in the right mood. My favourite kind of day is a slightly gloomy one, with maybe a patter of rain, where you need a little pick-me-up and don't mind spending the day inside little shops having a rummage. Already have a simple stylish outfit on, easy to take off and put on, and wear shoes that will go with anything.

The first two things to look for upon entering your chosen vintage/thrift store are texture and colour. When considering texture, aim for something a bit different, such as lace, sequins, velvet, chiffon or silk. With colour, be tasteful. Blacks and reds are timeless, and block colours are always effective.

When you've had a good old rummage (remember: never neglect the men's section as there is always potential for some darling shirt dresses), make your way to the dressing room. You love the dress – now it's time to see if the dress loves you. While it's fine to ask your friends' opinions, you should always trust your own instinct. This is when your creativity really needs to step in.

Your final decision should always be entirely based upon two questions: how did you feel when you had the dress on, and if you don't buy it, will you go home and regret leaving it for someone else to find? By then it will be too late.

Vintage pieces are the ones you will keep for ever; they are the ones that you will pull out of a trunk in your old age as you reminisce about the times you had wearing them. So choose your dress wisely, wear it with taste, take good care of it and cherish it, because as long as you love your dress it will love you.

You'll know that you look glamorous when men ask for your name and women ask for the name of your dressmaker.

HAIR and MAKE-UP

HAIR BASICS

YOU WILL NEED

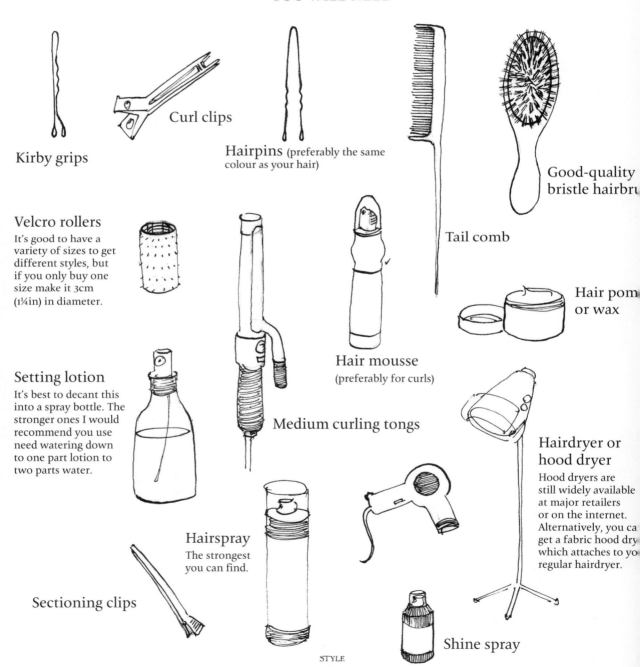

Kirby grips

Curl clips

Hairpins (preferably the same colour as your hair)

Tail comb

Good-quality bristle hairbru

Velcro rollers
It's good to have a variety of sizes to get different styles, but if you only buy one size make it 3cm (1¼in) in diameter.

Hair mousse
(preferably for curls)

Hair pom or wax

Setting lotion
It's best to decant this into a spray bottle. The stronger ones I would recommend you use need watering down to one part lotion to two parts water.

Medium curling tongs

Hairdryer or hood dryer
Hood dryers are still widely available at major retailers or on the internet. Alternatively, you ca get a fabric hood dry which attaches to yo regular hairdryer.

Hairspray
The strongest you can find.

Sectioning clips

Shine spray

WHAT YOU NEED TO KNOW

The secret to the styles on pages 276–289 is in the prepping of your hair. Unless you are doing a wet set, I recommend that you wash your hair the day before, as then it will be much more pliable.

When using rollers, or pin curling, always roll the hair horizontally as this gives your hair the most beautiful vintage curl. If you're having trouble making sure that the ends of your hair are wrapped securely around a roller or in a pin curl, use the narrow end of a tail comb to tuck the ends under the rest of the hair on the roller or into the pin curl. If you take your curlers out and you vaguely resemble a French poodle, don't panic! The secret to these styles is all in the brushing – lots of it.

PIN CURLS

If you don't have the time to use rollers, setting your hair with pin curls can have equally wonderful results. Apply a liberal amount of mousse to dry hair and follow the sectioning stages for the Classic Set (*see* pages 276–279) while your curling tongs heat up. Taking rectangular sections of hair no wider than 1cm (½in), pull the hair taut at a 45-degree angle. While holding the tongs horizontally, wind the hair around the tongs, making sure it is distributed evenly along the barrel. To avoid the dreaded 'fish-hook' effect so commonly experienced with curling tongs, gently release the tong clamp and slide the tongs along the hair until the ends are securely tucked in the clamp. Wind the hair under towards the head, rather than over. Hold the tongs in place for around 20 seconds then gently release the clamp and remove the tongs. While the hair is still hot, wind it around your forefinger keeping the curl horizontal and use a kirby grip to secure.

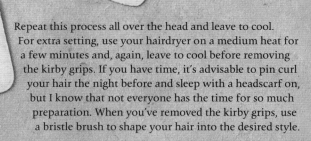

Repeat this process all over the head and leave to cool. For extra setting, use your hairdryer on a medium heat for a few minutes and, again, leave to cool before removing the kirby grips. If you have time, it's advisable to pin curl your hair the night before and sleep with a headscarf on, but I know that not everyone has the time for so much preparation. When you've removed the kirby grips, use a bristle brush to shape your hair into the desired style.

THE
CLASSIC
SET

This timeless style works on hair of all lengths and most types, and you can adjust the type of curl or wave you want by using different-sized rollers. There are various ways to achieve the Classic Set, with some people preferring to style their hair from wet and others from dry. There are those who prefer to use setting lotion and others who prefer mousse; some use velcro rollers and a hood dryer and others like to pin curl. It really is about experimenting and finding out what works best for your hair type and length and what kind of curl you want. The traditional method was a wet set with a hood dryer, which not only gives a better hold, but the whole process is ridiculously glamorous and fun, and that's just what us vintage girls are all about.

STEP 1 After washing your hair, blow-dry with a hairdryer until it's about 80–90 per cent dry. Spray your hair liberally with setting lotion all over and comb through to ensure even coverage. If any part of the hair is dry, it will set unevenly and potentially drop very quickly.

STEP 2 Part your hair using a tail comb into a front and back section from one ear to the other across the crown of the head. Divide the front section into two, keeping a side parting. The two front sections should be about the width of the roller you'll be using.

STEP 3 Starting on either side, take a rectangular section of hair about 1cm (½in) deep and, starting at a 45-degree angle away from the wrapping direction, wrap the hair around the velcro roller horizontally, rolling under, not over. Make sure that you hold the hair taut while rolling. Velcro rollers will generally stay in place themselves, but for extra security I use curl clips or kirby grips as well. Continue this process on both side sections, ensuring that all the rollers are horizontal and as close to your head as possible.

STEP 4 Part the hair at the back into two sections vertically and repeat the process until all your hair is set in rollers.

STEP 5 Now comes the easy part: spend 45–60 minutes (depending on the thickness of your hair) under a hood dryer. You can use this time to paint your nails, do your make-up, or just relax. For a set that will last for days, set your hair in the evening, sleep in your rollers (the things we do for glamour!) and wear a headscarf all day before taking the rollers out the following evening.

STEP 6 Make sure that you let your hair cool for about 15 minutes before removing the rollers. At this stage you will be wondering where your Lana Turner-style curls are, as you will be looking more like Shirley Temple, but fear not. Using your bristle brush, give your hair a good, thorough brushing. Now you may start to look like that French poodle mentioned earlier. Using the palms of your hands, apply a little styling pomade or wax through the lengths. Then, by brushing a little more lightly, start shaping the hair, even using your fingers, until you have achieved a look that you are happy with. Finish your style with a strong hairspray.

THE POODLE

The secret to Betty Grable's signature hairstyle is all in the preparation, and once that's done, it's easy. As mentioned with the Classic Set, setting your hair overnight gives a longer-lasting set so, if you can, pin curl your hair the night before you want to wear this style. If you don't have time, tonging your hair on the day will also work.

STEP 1 Apply some mousse liberally through the length of your hair and comb it through. Taking sections of no more than 1cm (½in), curl using your curling tongs and secure into pin curls with kirby grips. Unlike the Classic Set, for this style these sections do not have to be neat and accurate, just roughly all the same size. If you don't have the time to sleep in your set and have decided to style it on the day, just leave your hair to cool for about 15–20 minutes.

STEP 2 Remove all the kirby grips and divide the hair into four sections. The first is a horseshoe shape that starts from your temple, through the crown to the other temple. The remaining hair should be divided into three sections vertically – two side sections and a back one.

STEP 3 Using kirby grips and hairpins, start pinning the curls in the top section into place. If you need more volume, use your curling tongs and a little backcombing to give some extra shape. Make sure the curls are pinned in various directions.

STEP 4 Taking the side sections, backcomb gently at the roots from behind. Then twist them gently away from your face and upwards to meet the back of the top section and pin securely with kirby grips.

STEP 6 Finish your style with a strong hairspray, smoothing the sides and back with the palm of your hand, and don't be shy with the shine spray.

STEP 5 Bring the back section up to meet the top, smoothing with your bristle brush, and pin securely, trying to disguise the kirby grips among the curls. Arrange the hair of all four sections so that they all blend in, tonging the ends if necessary.

VICTORY ROLLS

Victory rolls are an iconic feature of 1940s hairdos. With this hairstyle, which is my particular favourite, you can do a full day's work, then dance the night away while looking as glamorous at the end of the evening as you did when you left the house.

The term 'victory roll' was originally used to describe a manoeuvre performed by fighter planes during World War II. Women adopted the term for the rolls of their hair in order to honour the soldiers who were fighting for their country.

This 'up-do' may seem tricky at first, but once you've mastered the basic roll it's a great style to experiment with. I adore my third central victory roll, and when I'm in the mood I sometimes create a fourth!

STEP 1 Divide your hair horizontally into two sections from ear to ear across the top of your head using a tail comb. Clip the bac section out of the way while you work on the front.

STEP 2 Apply some mousse to the front and divide it into three sections by creating two partings above the arch of your eyebrows.

STEP 3 Using your tongs, curl each side section upwards and pin into place while still hot. In this case, ignore the previous advice about curling under, because you will be victory rolling these sections, and pin curling first just makes it that little bit easier.

STEP 4 Divide the middle section into two, horizontally, across your head. Tong these sections away from the side you will be wearing your parting on, and pin into place. While the front sets, you can move on to the back.

STEP 5 Smooth the back with a little styling pomade or wax and divide horizontally into two sections. This style looks great with two back rolls, but it is easily adjusted so you have just the one.

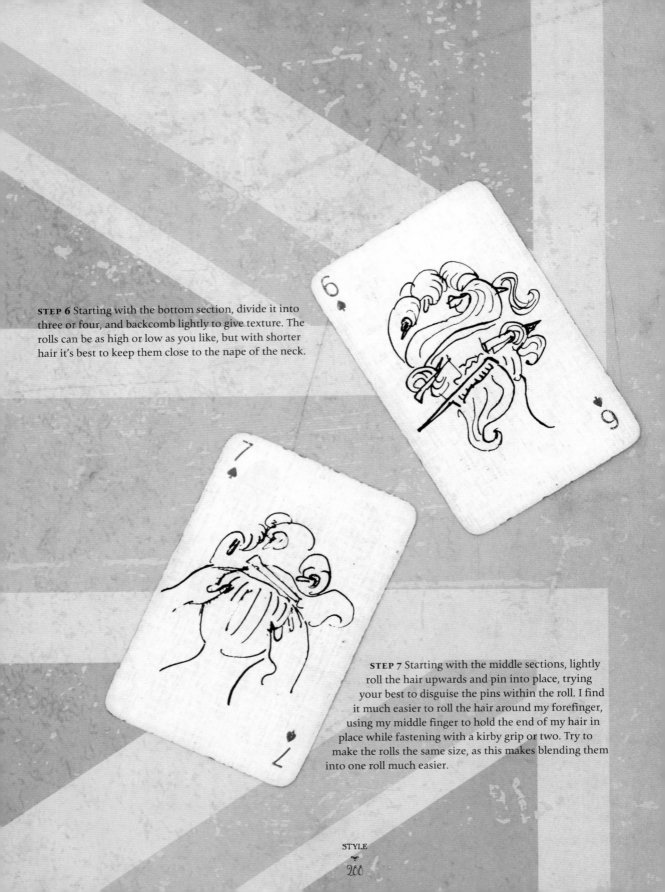

STEP 6 Starting with the bottom section, divide it into three or four, and backcomb lightly to give texture. The rolls can be as high or low as you like, but with shorter hair it's best to keep them close to the nape of the neck.

STEP 7 Starting with the middle sections, lightly roll the hair upwards and pin into place, trying your best to disguise the pins within the roll. I find it much easier to roll the hair around my forefinger, using my middle finger to hold the end of my hair in place while fastening with a kirby grip or two. Try to make the rolls the same size, as this makes blending them into one roll much easier.

STEP 8 (LEFT AND BELOW) Try rolling the end sections slightly diagonally, as this gives lovely detailing when the style is seen side on. Repeat steps 7 and 8 for the top section at the back.

STEP 9 Coming back to the front, remove the grip holding your pin curls in place and backcomb the first side section a little at the root to create volume. Then, using the thumb on the hand opposite to the side you'll be styling, wrap the hair around it, tucking the ends underneath while using kirby grips inside the roll to fasten it in place. You may like to practise this a few times while you get used to it, and you'll find it gets easier each time. When you're happy with your victory roll, finish with some hairspray, using the palm of your hand to smooth any stray hairs into place. Repeat this step on the other side section. Lightly backcomb the front top section from behind and, using your fingers, shape into a curl while pinning into place. Repeat this with the back top section, but bring the roll slightly further to the side and pin into place using kirby grips. There can be many variations of the Victory Rolls hairstyle, so just have some fun. Finish your style with hairspray and a spritz of shine spray.

Make--up and make-out

A flirty flick and a ruby lip is all it takes to make every day a glamorous one. Just have a look at the colour palette and follow these simple steps for the perfect vintage look.

Create a clean flawless complexion by covering blemishes and under-eye circles with concealer. Use green concealer to balance out red imperfections.

Use a liquid or cream foundation that matches your skin tone. Apply with a brush for even coverage. If using liquid, always squeeze on to the back of your hand first, to avoid going overboard.

Use an eyebrow pencil or angled brush and eyeshadow to fill in your brows. The vintage eyebrow is strong, sculpted and dark. The brow should start above the inner corner of the eye and extend past the outer edge.

Next, use a neutral eyeshadow to cover the entire eyelid before lining the socket crease with a darker brown. Use the palette to experiment with day and evening shades.

To create the liquid eyeliner flick, close one eye and draw as close to the lash line as possible in one swoop, extending beyond the edge of the eye to create the flick. You may find it easier to pull the side of the eye taut. 'Practice makes perfect' should be your mantra.

If you want a beauty spot use your eyeliner to do this, and experiment with positioning.

Crack a smile and dust the 'apples' of your cheeks with blush.

Use a loose or compact powder to finish off the look. This is an essential stage that will seal your make-up and complete your flawless face.

Next, use a black mascara to extend and curl your lashes – using curlers beforehand is optional. If it's an evening event, fake eyelashes are essential (*see page 292*).

To create the perfect pout moisturize your lips with balm. Next, carefully draw around the lips' edges with a lip pencil. Using a matching colour, fill in your lips with a brush and blend with the pencil. To make sure you won't get any on your teeth, suck your thumb and then pucker your lips on a piece of tissue to blot off any excess.

Job done!

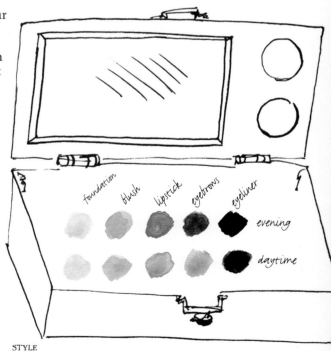

HOW TO APPLY FAKE EYELASHES

Fake eyelashes offer a great way to create a quick-and-easy elegant look for either everyday or evening make-up. You can look sophisticated or seductive with different styles of lashes, so experiment and find out which ones are best for you.

First, curl your natural eyelashes with an eyelash curler, so that they imitate the shape of your fake lashes. Also apply a bit of mascara so that your natural eyelashes will blend with the ones you are putting on. You can do this before or after you have applied the lashes. Carefully remove them from the box and bend them slightly so it will be easier to fit them on to your eyelashes. The glue is supplied with the lashes.

STEP 1 The lashes may need trimming at each end before you apply them. Compare them to your natural eyelashes to determine how much you need to take off. Trim them using a small pair of straight-lined scissors.

STEP 2 Put a small amount of glue on the back of your hand and run the base of each lash through it. Alternatively, run the tip of the tube of glue along the base of each lash.

STEP 3 Wait for around 15 seconds to allow the glue to become tacky.

STEP 4 You can apply the lashes using either your fingers or a pair of tweezers.

STEP 5 Moving from the outer eye towards the inner eye, slowly apply each lash as close to the base of your natural eyelashes as possible and press to secure.

STEP 6 Use a cotton bud to push the lash down towards your eyelash line if there is a gap between the two. Press the lashes in place for around 30 seconds, until secure.

STEP 7 For a natural, seamless look, fill in any gaps with liquid eyeliner or eye shadow. Fluff the lashes up with your fingers to create a flirty look, or smooth them down for a sultry look. It's as easy as that!

Male Grooming

For most of my childhood I was happy being a girl. I got to dress up and paint the faces of the ladies in my family... and sometimes the men, too. I didn't want to leave them out and felt that they were missing all the fun.

I was wrong.

Yes, girls get more choice and freedom to experiment, but male grooming is an art form of the highest order, and it's all in the attention to detail. It requires intelligence and thought and, when done correctly, looks distinguished, charming and effortless.

If your man is already ahead of the game, then skip over these pages and feel proud! If not, here is the Vintage Patisserie Male Grooming wish list.

Well-groomed hair

A man should never be without his Brylcreem. Try a 'short back and sides and long on top' for a 1940s look, or a neat and slicked side parting for a dashing 1920s gentleman.

Waxed moustache

Groom the moustache with a comb and twist it at the ends for absolute perfection.

Suit

This is one of the most important pieces in a man's wardrobe, and it should always be as expensive as he can afford. Of course, it's every man's fantasy to take a trip to Savile Row (or maybe every woman's fantasy) and have something tailor-made.

Jacket

It's vital to get a jacket that suits the shape of the body. Considering either double- or single-breasted, depending on build. The ends of the sleeves should always show the cuff and cufflinks, so these can be admired.

Trousers

Trousers should never be too long. A good cut will hit the ankle and show off an ample amount of sock when the gent is sitting down. There's also the danger of the horrible modern low waist, which is so ungentlemanly. The waist should sit comfortably above the hips with or without a belt. If in doubt, go higher – in the 1920s high waists were all the rage.

Waistcoat

This is an optional extra to a fabulously well-cut suit, although the older gent may laugh at the idea of not having a matching three-piece. In a more modern twist, textures and colours can be mixed, but beware – only the most fashion-savvy man can wear three different pieces. To be safe, always match two out of three.

Buttoned-up shirt
No self-professed gentleman would ever be seen without his collar and cuffs buttoned up. Colour and pattern are matters of personal preference, but coordination with jacket, coat and trousers should always be considered.

Vest
Most men will find wearing a vest under a shirt extremely useful. It allows for the tackling of instant DIY projects and car maintenance (for which every gentleman should be prepared) without the danger of unsightly shirt stains.

Braces
These optional extras look fantastic whatever the occasion, as well as doing the job of holding up your trousers, of course! Try matching the colour with the lining of your jacket, your socks or your cufflinks.

Tie
The knot should be neat and regular in size, with the back piece obscured from view. Tie clips are excellent for keeping everything in order, as well as adding some extra flair. A bow tie is another option, especially for more formal occasions, but beware the clown effect. Again, always remember to coordinate.

Handkerchief
This has traditionally been worn in the breast pocket of a suit and shouldn't coordinate with the tie – it's taking matching too far.

Cufflinks
Oh, how important these are! They are designed to keep shirt cuffs neat and tidy, and it's the attention to detail that makes a man look truly distinguished. Male jewellery is a difficult subject, but a man can be imaginative without the danger of looking garish when choosing his cufflinks.

Wristwatch
In this age of smartphones, many may say there is little use for a wristwatch. But a proper watch is as individual as the man himself, and is a constant symbol of preparation and organization. For the more flamboyant gent, there's always a pocket watch, which will never fail to grab the young ladies' attention.

Coat

The right coat is so important (especially in the great British weather) and must make a good first impression. If you want to have perfect vintage style, a man's coat should always be to the knee or longer, because then it cuts a dashing figure. Always consider the collar and fastenings, too, and make sure they're both comfortable and stylish.

Socks

It's very important not to forget these. A mismatched pair of socks is totally unforgivable, and if proper trousers are worn they will definitely be on show, so make sure that you have coordinated them to the rest of your outfit. The tragic ankle sock should never be seen on a man, and the most traditional gent may even go for a half hose, which finishes half-way up the shin.

Shoes

Gentlemen, here's a little secret. Women always look at a man's shoes on first meeting. It sets the tone for his entire outfit. So they should be stylish, of the highest quality and clean. Here is the Vintage Patisserie wish list:

Oxfords

These are the ultimate traditional men's shoes. They are plain and simple dress shoes, perfect for all formal occasions, made of leather and with simple 'closed lacing'. Gentlemen, if you're even *thinking* of wearing unlaced shoes with a suit, you need to be stopped now!

Brogues

Brogues are made from heavy leather and have a traditional pattern like a W on the front of the shoe, as well as small perforations. They tend to come in ox-blood, brown and tan colours, and are the perfect shoes for a casual or more formal occasion.

Tassel Loafers

These are a classic non-lace-up option, but beware of low-cut styles, such as a woman's 'penny loafer'. Those would look rather silly with your dashing outfit.

Chelsea Boots

This type of boot can be found with a traditional round toe or a more youthful severe point. It's all about personal preference. They are fantastic for all weather conditions and a country walk.

Hats

The vintage man will never look out of place wearing a hat. Short-brimmed fedoras will complement a suit and there's always the flat cap for more casual attire. Experiment to discover what suits you.

VINTAGE PATISSERIE THANK YOU

93 Feet East For allowing me to host my parties at your amazing venue which allowed me to grow my business! www.93feeteast.co.uk

ariotek For being the best web hosting company I've ever come across. Drew and Colin, you are both amazing! www.ariotek.co.uk

Barnet Lawson For being the best haberdashery I've ever been to. London is worth a visit just for you. www.bltrimmings.com

BBC and all the 'Dragons' Den' team For supporting me, mentoring me and being so kind! www.bbc.co.uk/dragonsden

Benefit Cosmetics For making the 'Big Beautiful Eyes' product. www.benefitcosmetics.com

Bethan Soanes For fitting into the Vintage Patisserie and researching your socks off! www.nothingbutbettinascarlett.blogspot.com

Carolyn Whitehorne For your support, encouragement and advice. www.toniandguy.com

Cass Stainton For 'getting' me.

Cate at Bitch Buzz For the loveliest write-up I ever got! www.bitchbuzz.com

Cliff Fluet For becoming my friend, for support, for encouragement, for understanding what I want to achieve. You are amazing. www.lewissilkin.com

Company Magazine For support. www.company.co.uk

DailyCandy For giving me my first bit of press! www.dailycandy.com

Dandy Dan Dan, thanks for thinking of me for every bit of press you can! You are a true gentleman. www.timeout.com/london

Dave at Bath Street Boxes For support and for our sexy packaging!

David Carter For being a loyal, eccentric dandy. Your creativeness has no limits. P.S. I plan to sell more books than you. :-) www.alacarter.com

Deborah Meaden For believing in me and giving me a stepping stone to grow my business. www.deborahmeaden.com

East London Business Centre For support and development from the start of the Vintage Patisserie. www.goeast.org

Eleanor Maxfield For commissioning the book! This would not have happened if you had not approached me drunk in a pub and said 'Here is my card'. You believed, you cared every step of the way and it's been lots of fun. I'm so happy that you've become my friend. Thank you!

Emma Perris For the wonderful massages you give, for support and being my mate! www.emmaperris.co.uk

Financial Times For support. www.ft.com/home/uk

Fleur Britten For being fabulous and supporting. www.fleurbritten.moonfruit.com

Fleur de Guerre For being a stunning pin-up and for being very talented. Please stop being so fabulous! www.diaryofavintagegirl.com

Fraser Doherty For being a business inspiration and making frightfully good British jam! www.superjam.co.uk

Gattina Cheung For allowing me to use your cake recipe along with being a very artistic inspiration. www.gattina.vpweb.co.uk

Geoff Oddie For designing every website I ever had and being amazing at it. www.geoffoddie.com/#/about

Grazia For support. www.graziadaily.co.uk

Harper's Bazaar For support. www.harpersbazaar.com

Hazel Holtham For being an amazing businesswoman and friend. Hazel, you are a beauty inside and out. www.ragandbow.com

John Moore For training me when I was 18, for helping at every step of the way, for caring and being a true friend. www.rsmtenon.com

Julie Caygill For help, advice and 'getting' it always!

Kathy at Past Perfect For having a brilliant company that sells amazing music! www.pastperfect.com

Katie For being the first to make a real business out of vintage. You are the leader, OH KATIE! Not to mention a bloody lovely lady. Thanks for supporting me. Let's take over the world. ;-) www.whatkatiedid.com

Kitty Kavanagh For continued support. www.kittykavanagh.co.uk

Lady Luck For being the first Vintage Dance Club in London and both being so fabulous. www.ladyluckclub.co.uk/top10.php?rad=on

Laura Cherry For being a huge part of this book. For working so hard and being simply so beautiful.

Lauren Craig For caring where your flowers come from, for being so talented and for being my friend. www.thinkingflowers.org.uk

Lauren Mittell If I could have 10 of you, there could be a Vintage Patisserie every town. Your hard work and focus never ceases to amaze me. Your beau makes the crowds at every party melt.

Leanne Bryan Thank you for caring and being so gentle and calming. I coul not ask for more from an editor. If you ever panic, I know we are in trouble!

Lian Hirst For having the best fashion PR label in town. Thank you for understanding and supporting and becoming an amazing friend. www.tracepublicity.com

Linton at The Fox For allowing me to host my parties, which allowed me to grow my business. And for nothing ever being any trouble. Linton, you are amazing! www.thefoxpublichouse.co.uk

Lipstick & Curls For inspiring hairstyles and being amazing and talented ladies. www.lipstickandcurls.co.uk

Luther Pendragon For support and being my sounding board. www.luther.co

MAC Cosmetics For creating the perfect look. What would a girl do withou her Ruby Woo? www.maccosmetics.com

Margaret at Vintage Heaven Margaret! You are the most amazing woman roam the planet. Your positivity fills my heart. Thank you for having the mo amazing business and filling in the gaps for my glass collection. I truly love you. www.vintageheaven.co.uk

Mehmet at Can Supermarket For everything!

Monica Chong For support, for becoming my friend and inspiring me with your creativity. www.cutlerandgross.com

Nathan King For advice and giving us your beauty for the front cover!

Naomi and Vintage Secret For support and love of vintage! www.vintagesecret.com

Nicholas Hill I love our chats!

Oasis For support and never getting bored with us. www.oasis-stores.com

Octopus team For all being so lovely and believing in this book.

Patrick at Value my Stuff For supplying the information for the props selecti and for being an inspiring businessman with style. www.valuemystuff.com

Paul Crook For support and for giving us dance.

Pete Katsiaounis For doing the illustrations for all my websites! You go beyond what a job is. www.inkandmanners.com

Piers Strickland For advice and support every step of the way. www.strickland-law.co.uk

Rare Tea Company For having a fabulous company and caring about it. www.rareteacompany.com

Samantha Vandervord For being the 'Dragons' Den' team member who believed and held my hand every step of the way.

Sharon Trickett For being incredibly hardworking, talented and utterly fabulo

Slinky Sparkles For being an amazing burlesque performer. www.slinkysparkles.c

Sophie Laurimore For sweeping me off my feet! Our business journey has j begun, but I feel like I've known you all my life. Thank you for being so amazi and hardworking. You 'get' it and I love you! www.factualmanagement.com

Stylist For support. www.stylist.co.uk

Sue and Jon For taking my cooking ideas and making them into reality. And telling me when something was silly! www.suehenderson.net

Susie and the Luna & Curious Team Susie, your creativity inspires me. You m see this in everything I do now. Thank you for bringing the Luna & Curious peo together and for supporting 24/7! www.lunaandcurious.blogspot.com

TeaSmith For having a fabulous company and caring about it. www.teasmith.co.uk

The Post Office, Roman Road For making me smile every day for the past 4 year

Time Out London For continued support. www.timeout.com/london

Uncle Roy's For selling edible flowers and having the most fabulous compa www.uncleroys.co.uk

Wella Hair For making the best hair products. www.wella.com

Yasia Williams-Leedham For your dedication and hard work, for your creativity and love of this project. I just love you so much that I hated telling y when I didn't like something! Thank goodness there were only a few. Thank yo for bringing this project together.

Yuki Sugiura For caring and being so talented and creative. The food photography makes me smile like a Cheshire cat. www.yukisugiura.com

ANGEL ADOREE THANK YOU

Gary Nurse For friendship, support and our deep conversations! Not only are you a beautiful man to look at, but the beauty goes much deeper.

Gossica Anichebe For laughter, love and friendship. Thank you.

Grandma, Nan and the rest of the ladies in my family For the love and kindness you've always shown me and for always looking fabulous!

Helen Carter For supporting and believing. Thank you.

Jake Sax and family For being the best sax player and my favourite ginger.

Jim Walker For living at the end of the garden! For being my dearest friend. For love and support and the proudness you have. I love you.

John, Julie and Katie Walker My second family! Thank you for the love I receive all the way over the pond. Not to mention taking me around all the vintage shops every time I came to visit!

Joseph Yianna For friendship and support and being so fabulous!

Judith Biffiger For sharing your world, inspiring me with music and love and being the gentlest, sweetest person ever!

Karen Pearson For being a friend and business inspiration. Essex girls rule!

Kate and Joe Skully For making me laugh till my sides split, for being bloody fabulous and for the love and support you have always shown.

LeaLea Jones For singing like an angel, for your open heart, for knowing that hard work pays off. Ms Jones, you are an inspiration to me and your peers around you. Hackney is a lucky place.

Leah Prentice For being the second Vintage Patisserie team member, and my mate, and causing me to laugh too many times. Mwah!

Lee and Fiona Behan Life's a pitch and I'll never forget it! Thank you for inspiring and supporting me.

Leo Chadburn I'll always remember how we met. I was sitting in a bar with my feet on the table and you approached me and said 'Your shoes are fabulous, would you like to party?' I'm actually not quite sure if that's how it happened, but that's what I'll go with. Twelve years of friendship and I love you so much. Your mum was proud of what an amazing son she has.

Mel Patel For being my mate and the only DJ I'd ever employ.

Mum and Dad For allowing me to be me. For showing me how to be open. For showing me how to love and give unconditionally. I'm the person I am because of you both.

Natasha For love and support.

Paul, Grandad and the rest of the men in my family For the love and kindness you've always shown me, thank you.

Sarah, Leroy and Henry One day the panda dress will be yours! Thank you for going beyond the call of friendship and believing.

Seymour Nurse When I see your name, I smile. Your kind words live in my heart and I'll love you for ever, Peter Pan!

Taj Cambridge We knew we would get here, we knew it was going to be OK, we had to remember what it takes to be happy. Me will always be we. Love you and thank you.

Tate and Anthony No one ever said it was going to be easy! We know this so well. Thank you for support on every level.

Val and Co at the Palm Tree For giving me the best nights of my life and for being such a lovely family!

Vicki Churchill Thank you for your creativity. Hope I get to see you soon.

Vicki, Young and Rosy For love, support and the party years!

I haven't met you, but I want to thank you for inspiring me and exciting me and being a layer of who I am today:

Her Majesty the Queen, Louise Brooks, Clara Bow, Greta Garbo, Bette Davis, Mae West, Vivien Leigh, Ava Gardner, Rita Hayworth, Ginger Rogers, Betty Grable, Lewis Carroll, Charles Worth, Gabrielle 'Coco' Chanel, Madeleine Vionnet, Elsa Schiaparelli, Christian Dior, Billie Holiday, Ella Fitzgerald, Doris Day, Sammy Davis Jnr (thank you for 'Mr Bojangles'), Nina Simone, René Gruau, Minnie Ripperton, Bill Withers, Curtis Mayfield, Stevie Wonder, Michael Jackson, Prince, Vivienne Westwood and Alexander McQueen.

On the following pages are some thank you cards you can scan and use. Your thank you letters may cross in the post. A thank you for coming, a thank you for having me, a thank you for 1000 layers that made the magic. 'Thank you' – two small words that weigh heavy with meaning. The circle is complete. I'm excited as I open my letter. I catch moments of memories and feelings. The invitation, the tastes, the smells, the laughter, the love. And I smile because it was good to receive… or give… I never know which one I enjoy the most.

...ele Mildred You inspire me with your beauty, love and endless creative ...ent and support. If you were not my core, I'd hate you for being so fabulous.

...son Coward My business and boys soulmate! Thank you for being so ...oud and supporting me every step of the way.

...dreya Triana For filling my life with music and love and endless praise! If I ...uld sing, I'd ask for a voice like yours.

...obby Nicholls and Lord Ian Thank you both for being the best party boys ...dy could wish for. It's never the same if you're not there. Bobby, I love you! ...u turn every vision into reality and even when I'm too tired to speak you ...d my mind.

...itta Dicke Support beyond what I deserved. Thank you for being there on ...ry level.

...ristina Lau I don't even know if I can put my thanks to you into words. ...at you have done over the 10 years that I've known you is be a true friend. ...u showed love and continued belief in me, teaching me how to bake, and ...ping with websites and business problems. I would have got here, but you ...de it easier and I love you so much.

...rren Whelen My oldest friend. Thank you for your love, support and ...inding me to stop every now and again!

...vid Edwards You are the perfect gentleman. Thank you for your endless ...pport and stunning photography (often for only a cupcake). I love you.

...ck Strawbridge From the moment I saw your face on a cupcake I knew you ...re the one for me. You truly are the most amazing man I have ever met and ...tell you every day until you believe me!

...zabeth Osbourne Thank you for caring and teaching me to read. Your ...mory has never been forgotten.

...ankyLou Franky, do you remember me? I miss and love you.

...ed and Katia Kunzi For taking me out of London and giving me the best ...mories I could wish for. I miss you and Switzerland.

...ia Facchnini (Mouthful O Jam) You slipped into our lives and it's like you ...re always here. Thank you. www.mouthfulojam.com

Thankyou

THANKYOU

INDEX

acknowledgements

PICTURE CREDITS
Fotolia.com adamgolabek
286–289 (flag), Alx 37 and
299 (frame), andersphoto
86, Fotographix 293 and
296–297 (background), Mila
Petkova 208 (background)

Getty Images Hulton
Archive 294

RECIPE CREDIT
The wondrous Caramelized
Pomegranate and Carrot
Cake on pages 140–141 is
reproduced by permission
of **Gattina Cheung** (http://
gattinamia.blogspot.com/)